P.E.T.S.™

Primary Education Thinking Skills Curriculum - 3 Updated Edition

Jody Nichols, Sally Thomson, Margaret Wolfe, and Dodie Merritt

Illustrated by Dodie Merritt

Cover by John Steele

Pieces of Learning
1990 Market Road
Marion IL 62959
www.piecesoflearning.com
CLC0503
ISBN 978-1-937113-67-4
Printed by McNaughton & Gunn, Inc.
Saline MI USA
10/2012

Acknowledgments

The authors of this book would like to thank the administrations of Illinois School Districts #47 and #424 for their support of the PETS™ program as well as the many primary teachers in whose classes these materials were field-tested.

A special thanks to Kerida O'Reilly, Ryan Shuflin, Carolyn Feffer, Beth Krabbe, Karissa Liddell, Joe Adducci, and Kate Gwozdz for the allowing us to use their unique Skedoodle concepts.

Many thanks as well to our families for their continued patience and support.

A note to our readers ...
Throughout the text, we alternate between "he" and "she" when referring to the students. Not only does this reinforce awareness that both boys and girls benefit from this type of programming, but it is also much more reader-friendly than always saying "he/she."

TABLE OF CONTENTS

PETS™ (Primary Education Thinking Skills)

DEFINITION

....is a systematized enrichment and diagnostic thinking skills program that can be easily integrated into an existing primary curriculum. *PETS™* serves the dual purpose of helping in the identification of academically talented learners and developing higher level thinking skills in students of all abilities.

PROGRAM RATIONALE

PETS™ follows the taxonomy outlined by Dr. Benjamin Bloom, presenting lessons in analysis, synthesis, and evaluation. These higher order skills are less emphasized in most primary curricula, yet students of all ability levels have shown interest in and understanding of these different types of thinking.

PETS™ also provides teachers with the opportunity to identify talented learners early in their school careers and to implement a curriculum which will best suit their special needs. This identification occurs in the classroom setting.

The format of the *PETS™* delivery system follows a modification of the Triad Model posed by Dr. Joseph Renzulli. The entire class is given the opportunity to experience the challenge of the thinking skills. Based on teacher observation and student interest, a small group of students is then given further opportunity to explore the thinking skills in a variety of in-depth activities. During the small group activities, the teacher is able to evaluate student potential further and to plan student programming accordingly.

PETS™ IN THE 21ST CENTURY

As educators in the 21st century, we are charged with educating students to be successful in a complex, interconnected world. This responsibility requires schools to prepare students for technological, cultural, economic, informational, and demographic changes.

PETS™ supports these thinking skills as outlined in the chart below. PETS™ also aligns with the Common Core State Standards as demonstrated in the chart on the following page.

PETS™ and the 21st Century Thinking Skills	Dudley	Isabel	Sybil	Yolanda	Max	Jordan
Inquire and think critically.	x	x	x	x	x	x
Apply knowledge to new situations, draw conclusions, and make informed decisions.	x	x	x	x	x	x
Share knowledge and solve problems ethically and productively as members of a multicultural world.	x	x	x	x	x	x
Demonstrate creativity, innovation, and flexibility when solving problems.	x	x	x	x	x	x
Pursue personal and aesthetic growth.	x	x	x	x	x	x

PETS™ and the Common Core Standards

Learning Areas	Standard	Common Core Initiative Site Location	Thinking Strand
	www.corestandards.org		
English Language Arts Standards	Read closely to determine what the text says explicitly and to make logical inferences from it; cite specific textual evidence when writing or speaking to support conclusions drawn from the text.	College and Career Readiness Anchor Standards for Reading »Key Ideas and Details #1	Convergent/Deductive
	Delineate and evaluate the argument and specific claims in a text, including the validity of the reasoning as well as the relevance and sufficiency of the evidence.	College and Career Readiness Anchor Standards for Reading »Integration of Knowledge and Ideas #8	Evaluative
	Prepare for and participate effectively in a range of conversations and collaborations with diverse partners, building on others' ideas and expressing their own clearly and persuasively.	College and Career Readiness Anchor Standards for Speaking and Listening »Comprehension and Collaboration #1	Divergent
	Demonstrate understanding of word relationships and nuances in word meanings.	College and Career Readiness Anchor Standards for Speaking and Listening »Vocabulary Acquisition and Use #5	Divergent
Mathematics Standards	Make sense of problems and persevere in solving them.	Introduction » Standards for Mathematical Practice	Convergent/Deductive
	Reason abstractly and quantitatively.	Introduction » Standards for Mathematical Practice	Convergent/Deductive Visual/Spatial
	Construct viable arguments and critique the reasoning of others.	Introduction » Standards for Mathematical Practice	Convergent/Deductive Evaluative
	Look for and express regularity in repeated reasoning.	Introduction » Standards for Mathematical Practice	Convergent/Deductive Evaluative
	Look for and express regularity in repeated reasoning.	Grade 1 » Introduction » Standards for Mathematical Practice	Convergent/Deductive Visual/Spatial
	Reason with shapes and their attributes.	Grade 1 » Introduction » Geometry	Visual/Spatial

PROGRAM OVERVIEW

PETS™ has a two-tier delivery system which is easily facilitated by the classroom teacher or a visiting specialist. The first tier focuses on whole class enrichment activities for the entire grade level population. The second tier activities are used in small group settings to challenge the more capable students.

PRIMARY EDUCATION THINKING SKILLS 1 introduces six characters, each with a special thinking strategy:

Dudley the Detective - deductive logic
Sybil the Scientist - analytical thinking
Isabel the Inventor - inventive thinking
Yolanda the Yarnspinner - creative thinking
Max the Magician - visual perception
Jordan the Judge - evaluative thinking

PRIMARY EDUCATION THINKING SKILLS 2 develops the thinking strategies further and introduces students to the terms convergent, divergent, visual, and evaluative thinking. The characters blend their thinking skills to work together to solve problems.

PRIMARY EDUCATION THINKING SKILLS 1 and **PRIMARY EDUCATION THINKING SKILLS 2** lay a strong foundation for **PRIMARY EDUCATION THINKING SKILLS 3** but are not necessary prerequisites.

In **PRIMARY EDUCATION THINKING SKILLS 3**, the characters continue to blend their thinking skills in a problem-solving format. More complex problems in logic, invention, visual perception, and evaluation develop these thinking strategies more fully in the young learner through stories and whole class games and activities. Small group follow-up lessons provide additional activities. These small group lessons stimulate students with high-interest, challenging activities, more intensive thinking games, and a variety of hands-on puzzles to solve. Detailed lesson plans are provided for the whole class and small group lessons.

Parallel to the instruction element of *PETS*™ is a two-tier diagnostic tool for identifying talented learners. A behavioral checklist that is used by the classroom teacher during the whole group lessons provides information about students who show potential for each thinking strategy. Students demonstrating outstanding aptitude during the whole class lessons, as recorded on the checklist, are invited to participate in the small group lessons. A more detailed checklist is used during the small group lessons to better identify student levels of talent and abilities.

The **PETS**™ **3** program is comprised of:

- -twelve lessons for the whole class
- -detailed lesson plans
- -twelve activities for the small group
- -diagnostic checklists

IDENTIFYING TALENTED LEARNERS

The primary classroom teacher has a very diverse population in both maturity and intellect. Some students will immediately appear talented in certain areas and other students need to be given opportunities to show their abilities. Before attempting to use the checklists, teachers need to understand the different characteristics and behaviors which indicate that a student might be talented in a particular area.

CONVERGENT THINKING

One characteristic of students who excel at convergent thinking is the ability to arrive at the correct answer intuitively. They tend to see the interrelationships between clues and defer judgment until all clues have been collected. In addition, students who analyze objects for various attributes as well as recognize flaws in reasoning demonstrate talent as convergent thinkers.

DIVERGENT THINKING

Those students who excel at divergent thinking are able to list many responses to questions or brainstorm many ideas. Not only are they fluent in their thinking but they may also exhibit flexibility. They tend to be original, giving off-beat and sometimes very humorous responses. These students can elaborate or expand upon an idea, adding intricate detail. An advanced vocabulary is sometimes displayed during the divergent thinking activities.

VISUAL THINKING

These students demonstrate a good memory for visual details. They may not be as verbal as their classmates and therefore may not have as much opportunity to demonstrate their talents during traditional classroom activities. These students often enjoy activities involving the mental manipulation of shapes and may respond well to visual images such as graphic organizers.

EVALUATIVE THINKING

The students who are able to evaluate and offer a solution that is based on valid considerations have an opportunity to shine during these specially designed lessons. The checklists support behaviors such as seeing more than one viewpoint, understanding criteria, and supporting decisions.

IDENTIFYING TALENTED LEARNERS DURING WHOLE CLASS LESSONS

The PETS™ program can help both classroom and specialty teachers identify talented learners in whole class and small group settings. The whole class lessons are the first tier in identifying talented learners. The ideal situation is to have two teachers in the classroom, one teacher presenting the thinking skill lesson and one teacher observing students' behaviors. If two teachers are not available, a parent volunteer or a teacher's aide may assist the classroom teacher. If this is the case, the teacher can help the aide by using key phrases to indicate that a student's name should be added to the checklist. For example, a teacher may say, *"Wow, Julie, that's a great way to use an earlier clue to see the new clue."*

Seven behavioral characteristics have been included for each thinking skill. The sets of behaviors vary from thinking skill to thinking skill. *PETS™ Behavioral Checklists* are provided in each unit as an easy reference for teachers. As a student is observed showing one of the behaviors, the teacher records the student's name in the appropriate box. If the student shows additional behaviors in the same category, the teacher can add check marks after the name. To differentiate between sessions, record each lesson's responses in a different color.

It is important for the teacher observing students to look beyond just the most vocal students who are the first to answer. All students need to be observed and questioned in order to give every student an opportunity to show her potential. There is a category on the *PETS™ Behavioral Checklist* to indicate students who show outstanding performance on class work. The *PETS™ Behavioral Checklists* also include an opportunity to list students who did not participate during the thinking skill lesson yet have shown the characteristics in other classroom situations.

It is essential for the teacher to remember that the number of talented learners in any one classroom may be quite small. The PETS™ program has been designed to identify this small population; do not expect the entire class to achieve mastery of the lessons. **All students will benefit from exposure to these higher-level thinking skills; however, the actual number of students demonstrating mastery level may be quite small.** That's OK.

Consider everything a child does to be diagnostic. Some children will respond enthusiastically to the intellectual challenges provided by the PETS™ whole class lessons while other children will not respond favorably. In each case, the reaction tells the teacher something about the learner.

At the end of one, two, or three whole class thinking skill lessons, the students who are talented in that thinking strategy will stand out as the teacher examines the *PETS™ Behavioral Checklist*. The students frequently listed on the checklist and listed in a variety of areas are the students who are invited to the small group lessons. When in doubt about a student's level of performance, include the child in the small group sessions and see how well he does – this is a time to be more inclusive than exclusive. Small group participants will often vary from thinking skill to thinking skill.

IDENTIFYING TALENTED LEARNERS DURING SMALL GROUP LESSONS

The second tier of the identification process is the small group lesson. The small group may consist of students from a variety of classrooms or a group from the same classroom.

The small group lessons are designed to provide further enrichment and opportunities for teachers to observe additional behaviors that identify talented learners. The small group lessons are not as structured as the whole class lessons, providing students with more opportunities for interaction and cooperative problem solving. These lessons are intended to be diagnostic rather than instructional. The teacher assumes the role of observer and recorder as students work independently through the activities.

Consider everything a child does to be diagnostic. Some children will respond enthusiastically to the intellectual challenges provided by the PETS™ whole class lessons while other children will not respond favorably. In each case, the reaction tells the teacher something about the learner.

The *PETS™ Small Group Checklist* on the following page is provided for record-keeping and note-taking during each small group lesson. Use one checklist for each group member and complete the student informaton on the checklist before the group meets.. The student's checklist is cumulative, so the same checklist is used each time a student is a member of a small group.

As this form is used to access and identify talented learners, any pertinent information or observations made during the small group lessons should be noted on the checklist. Not every characteristic is applicable to every lesson. At the end of the school year, the data from the *PETS™ Small Group Checklist* will give teachers information to help identify talented learners.

PETS™ Small Group Checklist

A Cumulative Student Record

STUDENT: SCHOOL: TEACHER:

	CONVERGENT			DIVERGENT			VISUAL/ SPATIAL			EVALUATIVE		
YEAR: DATE												
ACTIVITY + exceeds expectations ✓ meets expectations - below expectations												
CHARACTERISTICS												
Comprehends concepts												
Reasons independently												
Solves puzzles/problems successfully												
Sees inter-relationships/uses clues & criteria												
Uses alternative methods to solve problems												
Enjoys puzzles/problems with a twist												
Defers judgments												
Supports evaluations effectively												
Is fluent with ideas												
Shows flexibility												
Exhibits originality												
Elaborates with many details												
Exhibits curiosity												
Displays an advanced sense of humor												
Uses an extensive vocabulary												
Demonstrates task commitment												
Demonstrates leadership												
Retains information												

COMMENTS:

INCORPORATING PETS™ INTO FORMAL SCREENING AND IDENTIFICATION OF GIFTED & TALENTED STUDENTS

A PETS™ rubric has been included for school districts that intend to incorporate PETS™ into their formal screening and identification process. Used along with traditional standardized test scores, data from PETS™ program participation generates a more inclusive picture of the talented learners in a school. Performance by individual students in small group sessions can be quantified using the scoring procedure outlined below:

1. Initially screen the student population for students who participated in at least 75% of the small group opportunities over the course of the whole program as offered by the school district.
2. Levels reflect either the grade levels at which the program was offered or the level of the PETS™ materials being used (the red book being level 1, the green book being level 2, and the blue book being level 3).
3. Scoring samples:
   A. In a 3-year program, a student who participated in the Divergent small group sessions each year (3 points), demonstrating strong effective use of divergent thinking strategies and an attitude consistent with that of a gifted learner each year (18 points), would receive a score of 21 points for Divergent thinking.
   B. In a 3-year program, a student who only participated in the Convergent small group sessions at Levels 1 and 3 (2 points), demonstrating a strong effective use of this strategy only at Level 1 (5 points) and an attitude each year consistent with that of a bright child (4 points), would receive a score of 11 points for Convergent thinking.
4. Scores for each type of thinking are finally totaled together to produce a quantitative score for use in an identification process that necessitates the use of numbers.

PETS™ IN THE REGULAR CLASSROOM

Once students have experienced the different problem-solving strategies used by the Crystal Pond Woods thinking specialists through the PETS™ program activities, it is important for students to see how these strategies work for them in "real" life. Applying the language of these specialists within the context of core classroom curricula whenever possible makes concrete connections for students and anchors these concepts more effectively in their minds.

Use the *PETS™ in the Regular Classroom* graphic organizer (page 14) when mapping out daily lessons/activities:

- What are you teaching?
- What thinking skill/s will it entail?
- Which Crystal Pond Woods character specializes in those strategies?

PETS™ Rubric

Date:

Students	Divergent				Convergent				Evaluative				Visual				Total
	Level			Score	Level			Score	Level			Score	Level			Score	
	1	2	3		1	2	3		1	2	3		1	2	3		

RUBRIC

3	2	1	0
Small groups at all levels	Small groups at two levels	Small group at one level	No small groups
Strong effective use of this thinking strategy	Effective use of this thinking strategy	Minimal effective use of this thinking strategy	No effective use of this thinking strategy
Usually demonstrated attitude consistent with that of a gifted learner	Sometimes demonstrated attitude consistent with that of a gifted learner	Demonstrated attitude consistent with that of a bright child	Demonstrated attitude consistent with that of a good student

PETS™ IN THE REGULAR CLASSROOM

LESSON/ACTIVITY	THINKING SKILL/S	THINKING SPECIALIST/S
		❑ Dudley/Detective ❑ Sybil/Scientist ❑ Isabel/Inventor ❑ Yolanda/Yarnspinner ❑ Max/Magician ❑ Jordan/Judge

Notes:

LESSON/ACTIVITY	THINKING SKILL/S	THINKING SPECIALIST/S
		❑ Dudley/Detective ❑ Sybil/Scientist ❑ Isabel/Inventor ❑ Yolanda/Yarnspinner ❑ Max/Magician ❑ Jordan/Judge

Notes:

LESSON/ACTIVITY	THINKING SKILL/S	THINKING SPECIALIST/S
		❑ Dudley/Detective ❑ Sybil/Scientist ❑ Isabel/Inventor ❑ Yolanda/Yarnspinner ❑ Max/Magician ❑ Jordan/Judge

Notes:

In this unit, students are presented with the concepts of convergent thinking. Dudley the Detective's deductive logic is combined with Sybil the Scientist's analytical thinking strategies as students organize and reflect on a combination of clues to determine the right answers to a variety of puzzles.

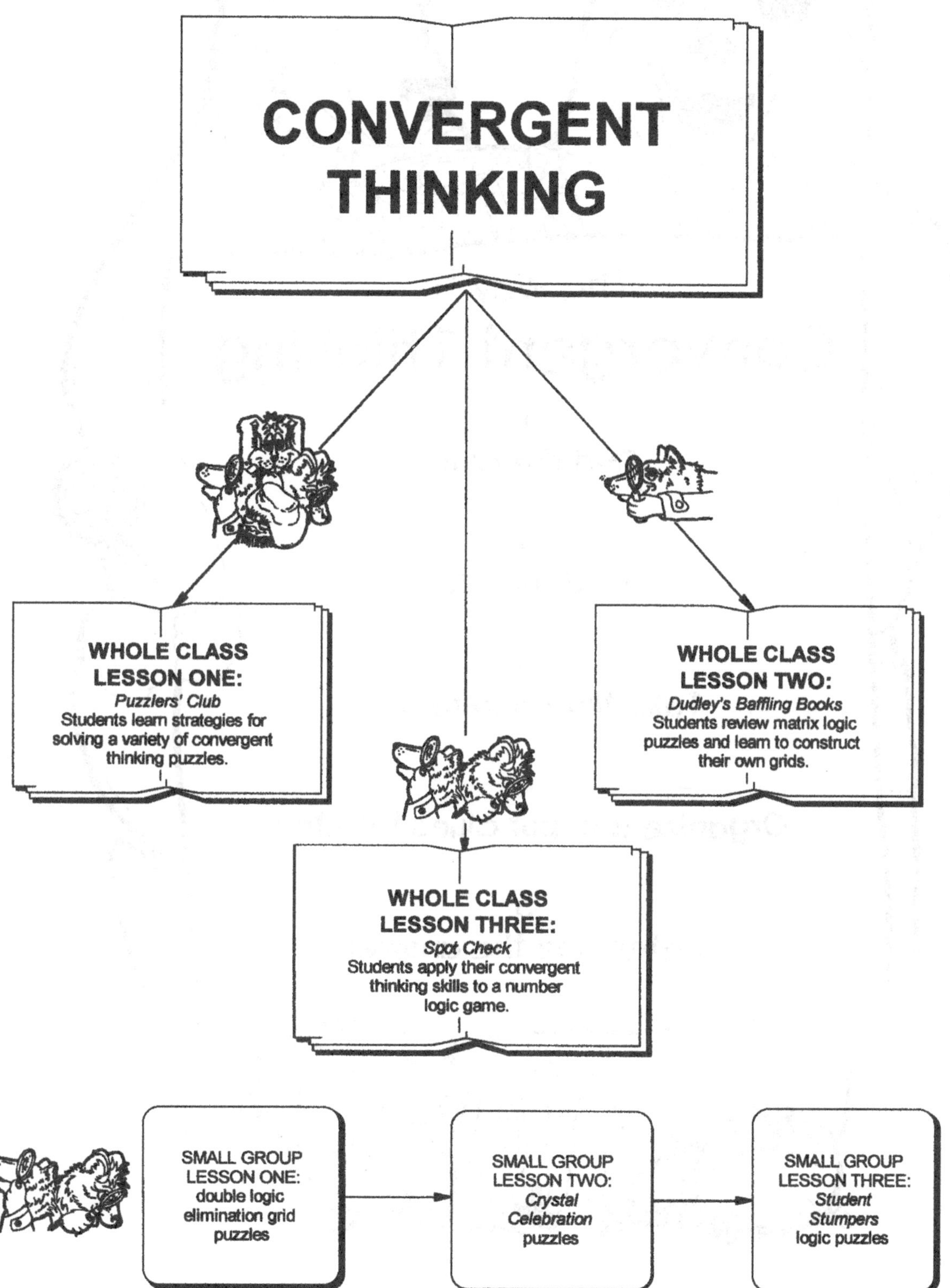

The Way to
Convergent Thinking
1.
Find the clues.
2.
Read the clues.
3.
Take time and reflect.
4.
Organize and put clues together.
5.
Determine the answer.
merritt

List names of students as each behavior appears. **Add checkmarks** after name if behavior is repeated. **Use a different color** of ink or pencil for each whole group lesson.	**PETS™** **Behavioral Checklist** **Convergent Thinking** (deductive logic/analysis)	Teacher ______________ Grade _____ Dates of whole group instruction: 1. 2. 3.

GRASPS CONCEPTS QUICKLY	**SEES INTERRELATIONSHIP OF CLUES;** PUTS CLUES TOGETHER; USES ONE CLUE TO DETERMINE ANOTHER
RECOGNIZES FLAWED REASONING	**DEFERS JUDGMENT;** CONSIDERS ALL INFORMATION BEFORE COMING TO A CONCLUSION
SEES ANSWERS INTUITIVELY WITHOUT INTERMEDIATE STEPS	**IS TENACIOUS** IN APPROACH; WORKS DILIGENTLY TO THE END
RETAINS INFORMATION FROM PREVIOUS LESSONS	**PETS™ CLASSWORK** INDICATES AN OUTSTANDING ABILITY TO USE THIS THINKING SKILL

I see these behaviors in these students regularly during class time as well:	These students did not stand out during the PETS™ lessons, but I see these behaviors during regular class time:	Notes:

DIAGNOSTIC NOTES • CONVERGENT THINKING

<table>
<tr><td>GRASPS CONCEPTS QUICKLY

♦ applies the process of elimination
♦ first to figure out correct answers</td><td colspan="2">SEES INTERRELATIONSHIP OF CLUES; PUTS CLUES TOGETHER; USES ONE CLUE TO DETERMINE ANOTHER

♦ combines information from various clues to determine the correct solution</td></tr>
<tr><td>RECOGNIZES FLAWED REASONING

♦ points out errors in logic</td><td colspan="2">DEFERS JUDGMENT; CONSIDERS ALL INFORMATION BEFORE COMING TO A CONCLUSION

♦ waits until enough information is gathered to work out the right answer
♦ avoids guessing impulsively</td></tr>
<tr><td>SEES ANSWERS INTUITIVELY WITHOUT INTERMEDIATE STEPS

♦ arrives at correct answer without seeming to use intermediate steps
♦ not an impulsive guesser</td><td colspan="2">IS TENACIOUS IN APPROACH; WORKS DILIGENTLY TO THE END

♦ works diligently to conclusion
♦ will NOT give up</td></tr>
<tr><td>RETAINS INFORMATION FROM PREVIOUS LESSONS

♦ shares knowledge accurately during review
♦ applies knowledge during activities</td><td colspan="2">PETS™ CLASSWORK INDICATES AN OUTSTANDING ABILITY TO USE THIS THINKING SKILL

♦ seatwork and/or challenge papers are exceptionally well done</td></tr>
<tr><td>I see these behaviors in these students regularly during class time as well:

♦ normally great convergent thinkers</td><td>These students did not stand out during the PETS™ lessons, but I see these behaviors during regular class time:

♦ normally great convergent thinkers who "hid out" during the PETS™ lesson</td><td>Notes:

♦ absentees
♦ new students</td></tr>
</table>

- *be generous — more inclusive than exclusive*
- *names can go in more than one box per answer*
- *be sure to add ✓s after names for multiple answers*
- *be sure to use different colors for each whole group lesson*

CONVERGENT THINKING
WHOLE CLASS
LESSON 1

PURPOSE

The purpose of this lesson is to review the characteristics of convergent thinking and to present the students with various problem-solving strategies.

MATERIALS

For projection:

– *The Way to Convergent Thinking* signpost
– *Favorite Toys/Glorbs*
– *Yolanda's Word Club*
– *What Works??*

For duplication:

– the story *Puzzlers' Club* to read aloud
– class set of *Dinner Dilemma/Cuddly Creatures Club*
– class set of *Waffits & Zamboids*
– class set of *Perplexing Patterns 1*
– class set of *Perplexing Patterns 2*
– class set of *Hidden Headgear*
– *PETS™ Behavioral Checklist - Convergent Thinking*

LESSON PLAN

1. If students have completed **PRIMARY EDUCATION THINKING SKILLS 1** or **PRIMARY EDUCATION THINKING SKILLS 2**, they learned that convergent thinking combines deductive logic and analytical thinking. The guidelines for convergent thinking are listed below and on *The Way to Convergent Thinking* signpost. The term **convergent thinking** as well as the following guidelines are presented in the story *Puzzlers' Club*:

- Find the clues.
- Read the clues.
- Take time and reflect.
- Organize and put the clues together.
- Determine the answer.

2. Read the story *Puzzlers' Club* aloud to students. Teachers will want to review the story ahead of time to be aware of the strategies used. The story provides four convergent puzzles to help develop problem-solving strategies as well as solutions to

these puzzles. Each puzzle's title is a heading in the story to make it easier to find the various puzzles and strategies. If students are able to discuss and solve the puzzles as a class, it is not necessary to read the entire story.

CHALLENGE PAGES

Dinner Dilemma/Cuddly Creatures Club
Waffits & Zamboids
Perplexing Patterns 1
Perplexing Patterns 2
Hidden Headgear

3. The challenge pages provide students with practice for the various types of puzzles introduced in the story. To provide the best opportunity for diagnosing talented convergent learners, the challenge pages should be done individually. Teachers may use the challenge pages after the story, as later seatwork, or as a Challenge Interest Center within the classroom. If challenge pages are sent home as homework or worked on in small groups, then use them as enrichment and not as assessment.

ANSWER KEY

Dinner Dilemma - Dudley

Cuddly Creatures Club - bunny, deer, moose - doubled adjacent letters

Waffits -1st, 2nd, 4th - 3 circles and 3 other curved shapes
Zamboids - 2nd and 5th - four digits on the hands

Perplexing Patterns 1 - c - b - a - b
Perplexing Patterns 2 - d - a - d - b

Hidden Headgear - blue
Sybil figured it out this way: Since there are only two yellow hats, if Jordan and I are wearing yellow, Max would know that his is blue, but Max doesn't know the color of his hat. Since Max is puzzled, Jordan must know that either Max, or I, or both of us are wearing blue hats. Jordan sees my hat, but he still doesn't know the color of his own. If my hat were yellow, Jordan would know that his own must be blue. Therefore, since he doesn't know his color, MY hat must be blue.

DIAGNOSTIC NOTES

During this lesson, the teacher and observer will be looking for students who display specific characteristics. These students may then be invited to the small group sessions for additional activities. Some teachers explain the structure of the **PRIMARY EDUCATION THINKING**

SKILLS curriculum to the students before actually starting the lessons. During the explanation, the teacher might point out to students the importance of volunteering during the lessons as this is the main opportunity for the teachers to observe what the students are thinking.

Look for the characteristic behaviors and responses listed on the *PETS™ Behavioral Checklist - Convergent Thinking*. There is an overlap of characteristics between the units and certain traits will show up throughout the curriculum. The following is a short summary of what to look for in student behaviors and responses for Convergent Thinking, Whole Class Lesson 1:

GRASPS CONCEPTS QUICKLY - Look for students who quickly understand and use the process of logical elimination. List the students who are the first to figure out the correct answers.

SEES INTERRELATIONSHIP OF CLUES - Note students who combine information from various clues in order to determine the correct solution.

RECOGNIZES FLAWED REASONING - Look for students who point out errors in logic.

DEFERS JUDGMENT - Look for students who wait until they have gathered enough information to figure out the correct answer. These students avoid guessing impulsively.

SEES ANSWERS INTUITIVELY - Some students who are excellent deductive thinkers are unable to verbalize how they figured out the answer. Note students who arrive at the correct conclusions without seeming to use the intermediate steps.

IS TENACIOUS - In addition to working diligently to the end of the activities, look for students who want to work on convergent-style activities. An enthusiasm towards this type of problem often indicates an ability to solve the problems.

RETAINS INFORMATION – When reviewing ideas from earlier lessons, look for students who clearly recall the concepts and then effectively apply them to the current lesson's activities. While many children may grasp concepts "in the moment" of the instructional lesson, these students exhibit the significant ability to retain and apply new learning across time.

Dinner Dilemma/Cuddly Creatures Club, Waffits & Zamboids, Perplexing Patterns 1, Perplexing Patterns 2, and ***Hidden Headgear***

Most important in the identification portion of this lesson will be those students who are able to complete these challenge pages correctly and independently. Note students who correctly solve the variety of puzzles. If a student has a specific strength in one type of puzzle, note that as well.

Puzzlers' Club

It was a fine summer evening in Crystal Pond Woods for the first meeting of the Puzzlers' Club. Everyone was there. Dudley the Detective was the leader of the Puzzlers' Club, and he prepared to welcome all of the great thinkers who were arriving with their favorite puzzles. Sybil the Scientist and Yolanda the Yarnspinner sat down next to each other ready to challenge the group. Max the Magician had his black hat on and a mischievous grin on his face. Jordan the Judge proudly perched on a low limb of Isabel the Inventor's oak tree, which stood tall right next to **The Way to Convergent Thinking** signpost, a prominent marker in the Woods.

"Welcome, one and all, to tonight's meeting of the Puzzlers' Club," announced Dudley. "A new member has joined our group. Please welcome Rosalyn Robin."

The puzzlers welcomed Rosalyn Robin with a hearty round of applause. Rosalyn nervously bowed a thank-you to the group.

Noticing her nervousness, Sybil said, "Don't worry, Rosalyn. Solving puzzles is so much fun that you're going to love being part of the Puzzlers' Club."

"You are all such great thinkers; I just don't know if I'll be able to keep up with you!" exclaimed Rosalyn.

"Why don't you review with Rosalyn just how we go about solving puzzles?" suggested Jordan to Dudley.

"That's a great idea!" replied Dudley. "We start with a mystery or a problem or a puzzle to solve. We're looking for the right answer by using **convergent thinking**. Convergent thinking combines analysis with deductive logic. Why don't we take a look at **The Way to Convergent Thinking** signpost to get an idea of how the process works?"

*(Project **The Way to Convergent Thinking** signpost.)*

Dudley continued, "To solve a mystery or puzzle, the first thing we must do is **find** clues that will help us. Then, of course, we have to **read** each clue so we can analyze it for important information. Next, we must carefully **reflect** on those clues. Sometimes, it's necessary to re-read and repeat the reflection step several times! After that, we **organize and put the clues together**. Then, finally, we are ready to use the information from our clues to **determine the one right answer** that solves our mystery or puzzle! Do you understand the process we'll be using tonight, Rosalyn?"

Rosalyn smiled thinly. "I think so. You're a good teacher. You make it sound very clear-cut."

Jordan looked wisely down on the group from his high perch. "Rosalyn, now are you ready to give the puzzles a try?"

"I think I am, if you're all willing to help me through them," Rosalyn replied.

(The remainder of the story provides puzzles and strategies for solving those puzzles. Teachers may continue the story with the characters modeling the strategies for solving the puzzles or may choose to project the activities and work through them as a class.)

Favorite Toys

"Then who wants to begin this evening's round of fun?" asked Jordan.

Dudley was eager. "I've got a good one that occurred to me just this week when you and Yolanda and I were playing together," Dudley said to Jordan.

*(Project **Favorite Toys** and read it aloud to students. Pause to give students an opportunity to think about the puzzle then solicit any ideas*

students can offer. Continue with the story if they are unable to solve the puzzle and further direction is needed. Otherwise skip to the next puzzle.)

"I know the answer!" shouted Isabel. "The clues are clear in my head!"

Max commented, "I am very visual. I'd like to collect these clues in an organized manner." He used his wand to write **Dudley**, **Jordan**, and **Yolanda** in the dirt. Then he added two more columns.

(Write the following on the board.)

Dudley	*jacks*	*yo-yo*
Jordan	*dominoes*	*yo-yo*
Yolanda	*dominoes*	*jacks*

"Now let's think about the clues. If Dudley says that none of them likes the toy that begins with the first letter of their names, then Dudley doesn't like to play with dominoes. He could play with jacks or the yo-yo."

"And Jordan's favorite would be the dominoes or the yo-yo and Yolanda's would be the dominoes or the jacks," chimed in Isabel.

Rosalyn spoke up shyly, "I see what you've done so far, but now I'm stumped. I don't see any more clues."

"You need to read the words carefully," cautioned Yolanda. "The next sentence says that the yo-yo player agrees with Dudley. That means Dudley can't be the yo-yo player either because he wouldn't agree with himself."

Sybil studied the chart over Max's shoulder. "Then let's cross out **yo-yo** on Dudley's list in the second column. And since Yolanda can't like the yo-yo best, that means Jordan must."

*(Cross out **yo-yo** in Dudley's row and circle **yo-yo** in Jordan's row.)*

Rosalyn chirped, "That means Jordan couldn't like the dominoes, and so Yolanda must! That means, I think, that Dudley likes jacks!"

*(Circle **jacks** for Dudley and **dominoes** for Yolanda.)*

"Brilliant deduction and excellent teamwork!" exclaimed Dudley. "On to the next puzzle!"

Glorbs

Sybil said, "I got my idea for tonight's puzzle from studying some strange creatures I found under a log in the woods this week. I've called them Glorbs."

*(Project **Glorbs** and read it aloud to students. Give students an opportunity to think about and solve the puzzle. If instruction is needed, continue with the story. Otherwise skip to the next puzzle.)*

"Wow!" exclaimed Rosalyn. "This one is really a stumper!"

Max smiled. "This puzzle is very visual. I think I can spot the differences. Let's find the clues. What do all of the Glorbs have in common?"

"Hmmm," pondered Dudley. "For one thing, they all have on a hat."

"Yes, that's true," agreed Jordan. "They also seem to have four feet, unlike my bird friends."

"There is hair sticking out from under their hats," noticed Isabel.

“They each have two eyes,” added Rosalyn, “but their mouths are all different and so are their body shapes.”

Max observed, “In the second row, there are also creatures with hats. It can’t be only the hats that make a Glorb a Glorb.”

“Some of them also have four feet and some have hair,” added Isabel. “And they all have two eyes. It can’t be any of these things by themselves that make them Glorbs.”

“Wait a minute!” exclaimed Max. “What if a Glorb has to have four feet, hair AND a hat to make it a Glorb?”

Rosalyn studied the last row. “In that case, numbers 1 and 3 would be Glorbs.”

Sybil smiled at Rosalyn proudly. “Exactly right,” she said. “You’re really a full-fledged member of the club now.”

Yolanda’s Word Club

Yolanda piped up next. “My puzzle is very similar to yours, Sybil, except that it uses words, of course.”

*(Project **Yolanda’s Word Club** and read it aloud to students. Give students an opportunity to think about and solve the puzzle. If instruction is needed, continue with the story. Otherwise skip to the next puzzle.)*

“A similar puzzle, all right,” agreed Max, “but much more difficult for me. I presume the words in the first shape have something in common, but I certainly cannot see what that might be.”

“Never fear - persevere,” coaxed Yolanda. “Try comparing the words in both of the first two shapes.”

Max and all the friends studied the words closely. "The first group has **o**'s in them, except for **three**," observed Sybil. "However, **look** has **o**'s in it, and that's in the second group."

"Most of them end in a consonant, but **three** ends with a vowel. And the second group all begin and end with consonants, so that can't be the clue," said Dudley.

Yolanda urged again. "Try thinking of the first group as a word club. What is the rule that allows them to be in the club when the second group of words cannot be in the club?"

"It's not the number of letters," said Rosalyn, "because there are words in both groups with the same number of letters."

Suddenly Jordan, from high on his limb, hooted, "What happens if we rearrange the letters in the words?"

Max's eyes lit up. "That's it!" he shouted. "The first group of words can be rearranged to make other words! **Not** can be rearranged to make **ton**, **stop** makes **pots**, **three** makes **there, words** makes **sword,** and **form** makes **from!** No words in the second group can do that."

"Words that can rearrange their letters to make other words are called anagrams," Yolanda said, savoring the feel of the word anagram on her tongue. "You've puzzled it out again! Now tell me which of these other words can be members of my word club." Yolanda pointed to the words at the bottom of the page.

"I know! Exclaimed Dudley. "The correct answers would be **note** because its letters can be rearranged to spell **tone** and **kids** which can be changed to **skid**."

What Works??

"Now it's my turn," said Max.

*(Project **What Works??** and give students an opportunity to think about and solve the puzzle. If instruction is needed, continue with the story.)*

"What do we do with this?" asked Isabel.

"Figure out which figure correctly fills the blank spot in each row," instructed Max, smiling at Yolanda for his own little wordplay.

Sybil studied the first row of figures for clues. "The triangle's numbers move in each shape," she observed to the group.

Dudley agreed. "It's as if the triangle is tumbling over clockwise. And if that were the case, the letter **a** triangle would correctly show the numbers for the triangle in the blank spot. That one was fairly easy, but the next one looks tougher."

The group of friends studied the second problem closely. "What are the clues?" Sybil asked. Then she answered her own question. "Each shape has a circle at the top and bottom. That always stays the same. But the triangle in the middle is sometimes black and sometimes white. It alternates."

Isabel added, "Another clue would be the square that moves from the middle to the top, then to the bottom and then back to the middle."

"Using Sybil's clue, the correct answer shape should have a dark triangle," observed Dudley, using his best detective thinking. "That eliminates **a** and **c**. And adding Isabel's clue, the square should be positioned at the top."

"Only answer **b** has both the correct criteria," Jordan announced.

"Bravo!" cried Max. "Can you be so astute with the third problem?"

"I think this one is easier," spoke up Rosalyn, "although I know I'm new to the club. This one looks as if the two shapes are moving to overlap one another, sliding along by inches. That would mean that they would have completely swapped positions by the blank space, and answer **c** would be my deduction."

"You're very bright, Rosalyn!" approved Dudley. "My deduction concurs with yours. How do you feel about the 4th one?"

Rosalyn studied the figures. "Well, each one is a star, like those overhead in Crystal Pond Woods."

"True," observed Sybil, "but none of them is quite the same. Each of these stars has a piece missing."

"You're right!" exclaimed Isabel. "The missing piece seems to move clockwise around the pentagram."

Jordan stopped studying the stars overhead to look at the star in the puzzle. "A very wise observation, Isabel. The pentagram with the correctly placed space for the blank spot would have to be..."

"**D**!" shouted all the puzzlers together.

Rosalyn was sorry that the puzzles were over. She could hardly wait for the next meeting of the Puzzlers' Club. She would have her own puzzles to bring, which she was sure would stump everyone at the club meeting.

Favorite Toys

Dudley, Yolanda, and Jordan were playing with their favorite toys — dominoes, yo-yo's, and jacks.

"Did you notice," commented Dudley, "that these toys begin with the same letters as our names, but that none of us like best the toy with the first letter of our *own* name?"

"That's true," agreed the yo-yo player.

Who likes which toy best?

Glorbs

These are Glorbs:

None of these are Glorbs.

Which of these are Glorbs?

1. 
2. 
3. 
4. 

What makes a Glorb be a Glorb?
How will you know a Glorb when you see one?

Yolanda's Word Club

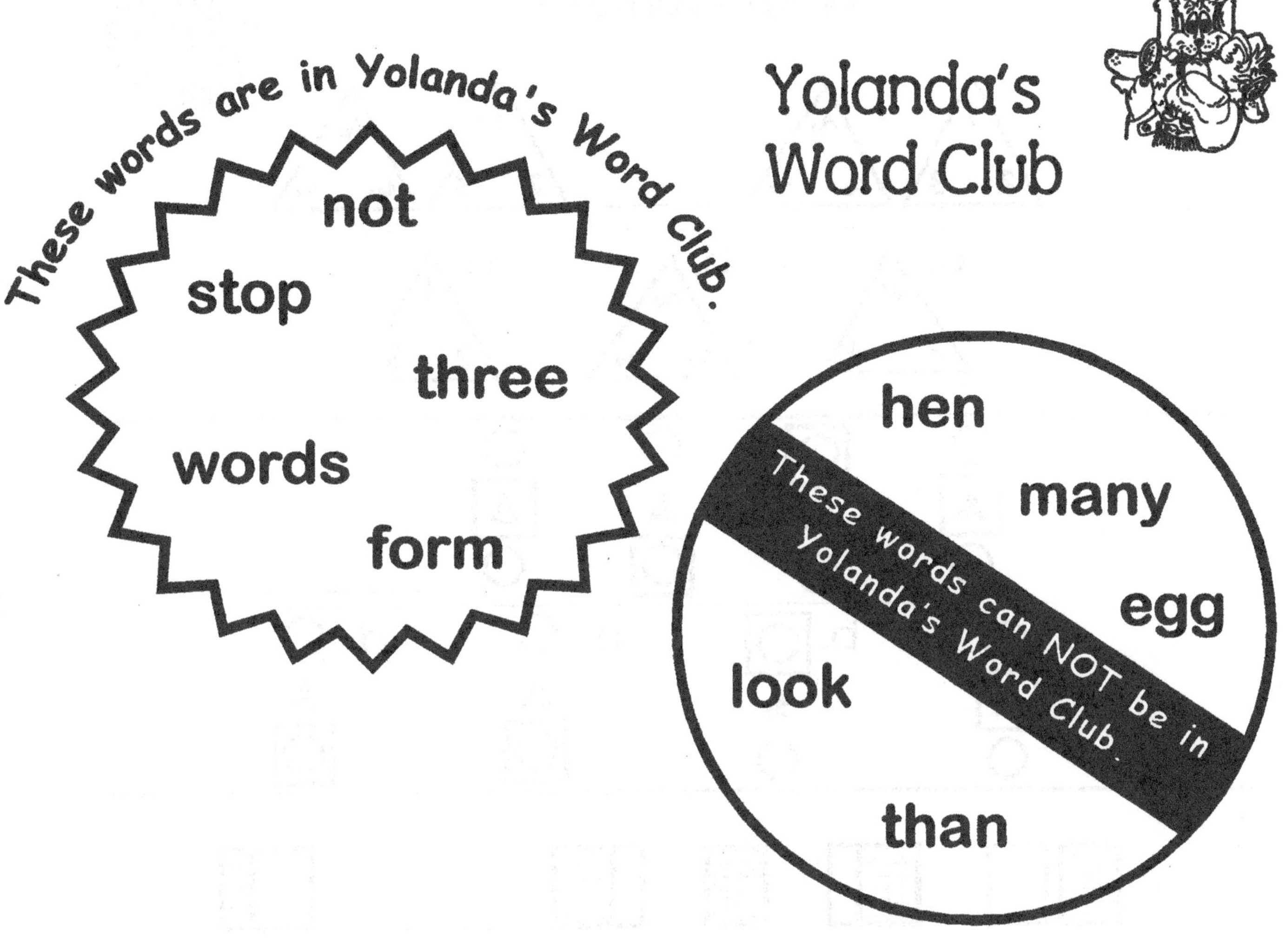

Which of these words below can be members of Yolanda's Word Club? Why?

card **knot**

seem **note** **kids**

dots **frog**

What Works??

1.

1 2 3 — ____ — 1 2 3

a. b. c.

2.

____

a. b. c. d.

3.

____

a. b. c. d.

4.

____

a. b. c. d.

Name ______________________________

Dinner Dilemma

Yolanda is having a dinner party tonight. Jordan, Isabel, Dudley, and Sybil are all seated along one side of a long table.

Dudley was seated next to Sybil, but **not** next to Jordan.

If Jordan is not seated next to Isabel, then who is?

Cuddly Creatures Club

These creatures are in this club:

squirrel
kangaroo
rabbit
kitten
raccoon

These creatures can NOT be in this club.

spider
eagle
hamster
bear
pony
lion
chicken
snake

Which of these other creatures can join this club?

bunny
dog
moose
owl
turtle
penguin
tiger
deer
camel
elephant

Circle the ones that can join the club.

Explain why: ______________________________

Name ______________________________

Waffits & Zamboids

These are Waffits.

These are not Waffits.

Which of these are Waffits? Circle them.

How do you recognize a Waffit?	Draw your own Waffit here.

These are Zamboids.

These are not Zamboids.

Which of these are Zamboids? Circle them.

How do you recognize a Zamboid?	Draw your own Zamboid here.

Name ______________________________

Perplexing Patterns 1

1.   ______

a.  b. c. d.

2. 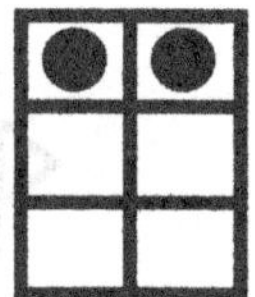 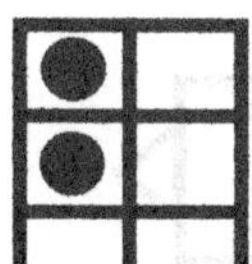 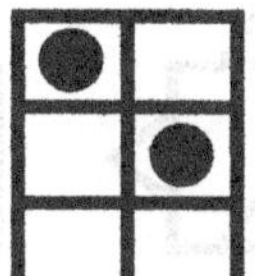 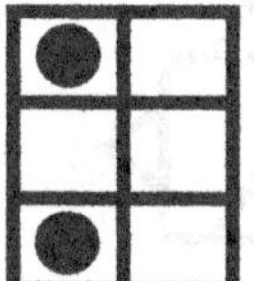 ______  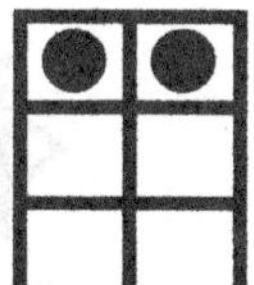

a. 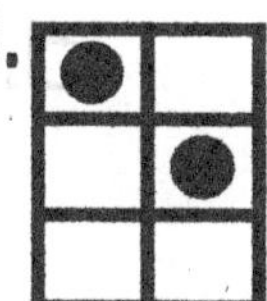 b. 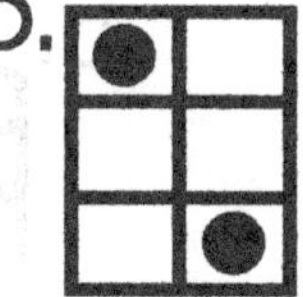 c.  d.  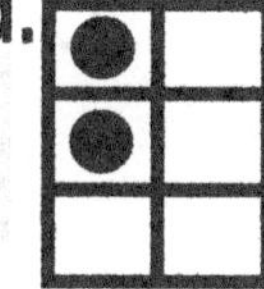

3.  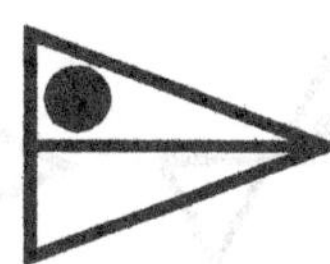  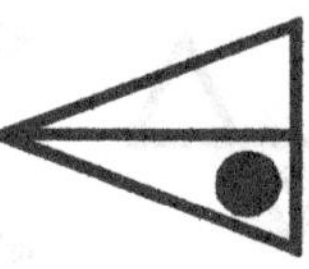  ______

a. 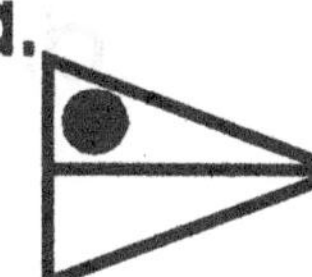 b. 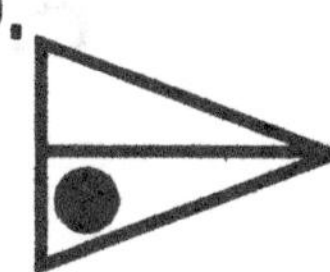 c.  d. 

4.     ______  

a.  b.  c.  d. 

Name ____________________

Perplexing Patterns 2

1.

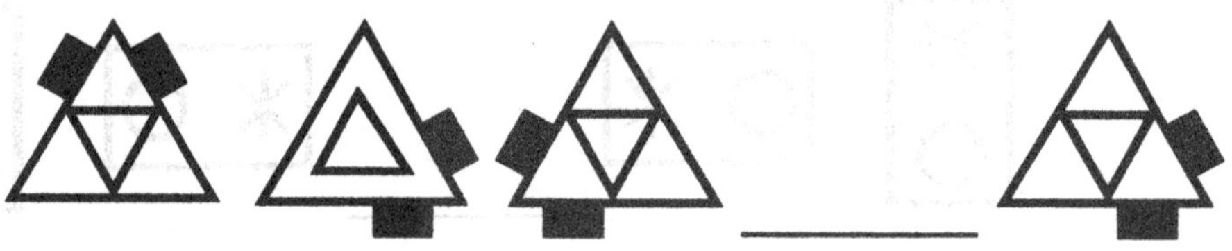

a. b. c. d.

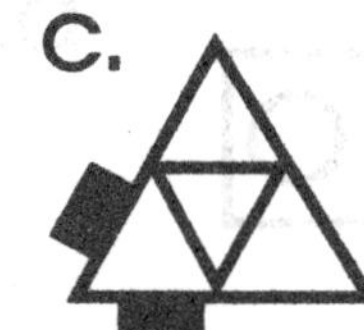

2.

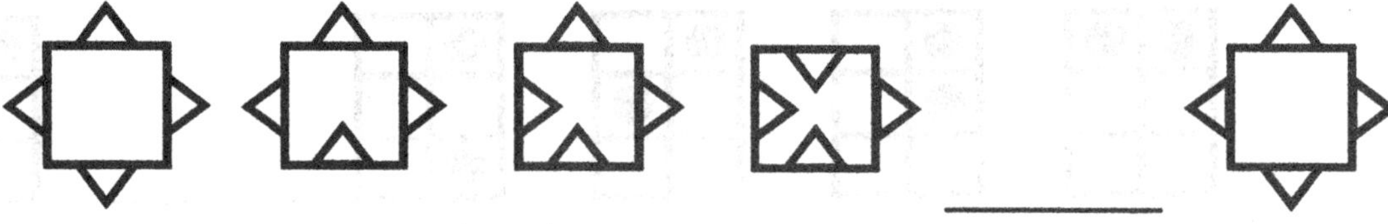

a. b. c. d.

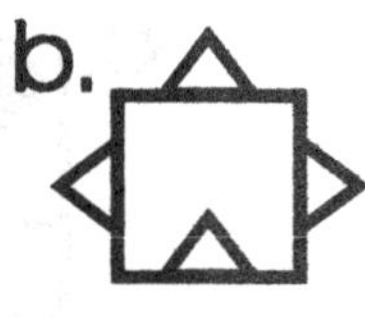

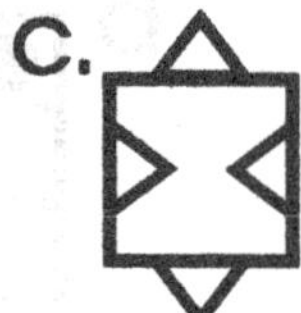

3.

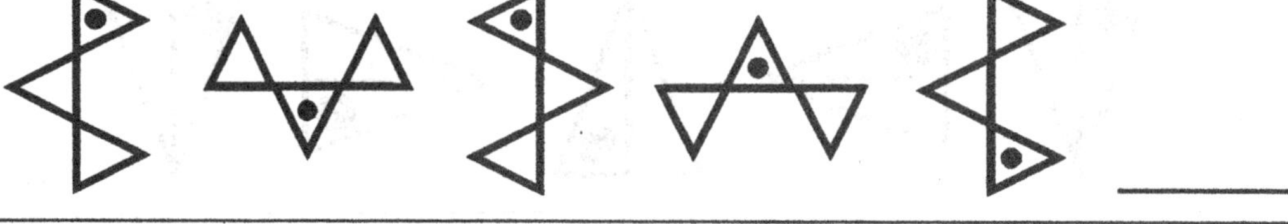

a. b. c. d.

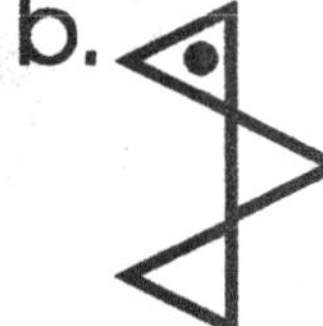

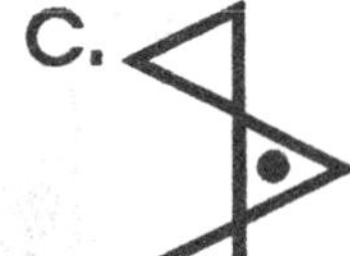

4.

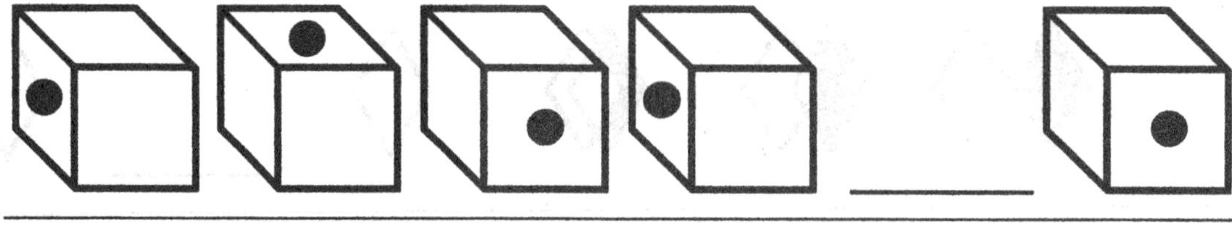

a. b. c. d.

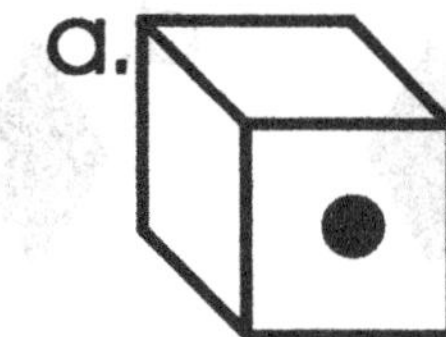

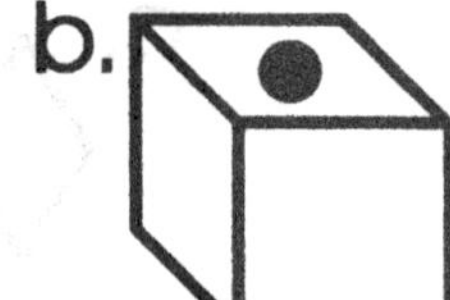

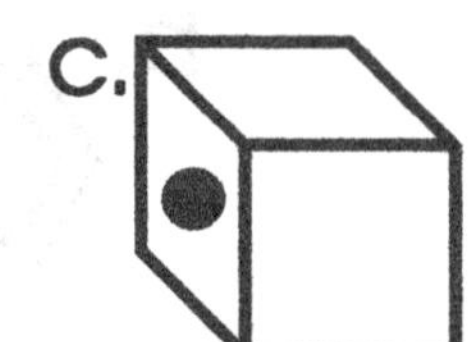

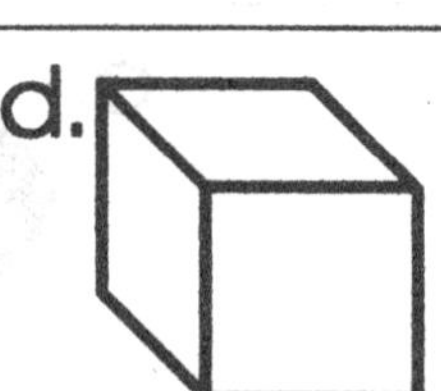

Name ______________________________________

Hidden Headgear

One evening at the campfire, Dudley the Detective pulled out a bag with a mysterious bundle inside. "In this bag," he told his friends, "are five hats. Two are yellow and three are blue. Now I want three volunteers for a serious detective puzzle."

Jordan, Max, and Sybil quickly raised their hands. Dudley had them sit facing each other. Then he told them to close their eyes while he placed a hat on each of their heads.

"Each of you must guess the color of the hat on your own head. You may not look in the pond for your reflection , but you must use your deductive thinking skills. You may, of course, look at the hats on the other two heads."

Max looked at both of his friends and the hats on their heads. "But I can't tell what color hat I'm wearing," he said in a puzzled voice.

Jordan agreed as he looked wisely around that he couldn't tell the color of his hat either.

Sybil smiled broadly and instantly blurted, "Then I DO know the color of *my* hat!"

What color hat was Sybil wearing?

How did she know?

CONVERGENT THINKING
WHOLE CLASS
LESSON 2

PURPOSE

The purpose of this lesson is to reinforce the concepts of deductive logic and to review how to use a logic elimination grid to organize clues into a visual representation of a logic problem.

MATERIALS

For projection:

– *The Way to Convergent Thinking* signpost
– *Dudley's Baffling Books Logic Elimination Grid*
– *Hide 'N Seek*

For duplication:

– the story *Dudley's Baffling Books* to read aloud
– class set of *Hide 'N Seek*
– class set of *Contest Conundrum*
– class set of *Dudley's Daily Schedule*
– *class set of The Missing Biscuit*
– *PETS™ Behavioral Checklist - Convergent Thinking*

LESSON PLAN

1. Review with students the guidelines for convergent thinking using *The Way to Convergent Thinking* signpost:

- Find the clues.
- Read the clues.
- Take time and reflect.
- Organize and put the clues together.
- Determine the answer.

2. Read the story *Dudley's Baffling Books* aloud to students. The following strategies for solving a logic elimination puzzle are introduced in the story:

- Logic elimination grids are a way to organize information from the clues.
- Each column and row is labeled with information from the puzzle.
- An **X** means that a pair of items **do not** go together.
- An **O** means that a pair of items **do** go together.
- To mark an appropriate cell, line up the correct column with the correct row,

and find the cell where these intersect.

- Clues that do not make sense right away need to be reflected upon until they do make sense in the puzzle.

- When the puzzle is finished, each row and each column should have exactly one **O** in it.

- The result of the grid shows the one correct answer to the question posed by the logic puzzle.

3. Some students may be able to determine the correct answer without seeming to use the intermediate steps. Although this should be noted on the *PETS™ Behavioral Checklist - Convergent Thinking*, it is important for the teacher to continue the lesson so all students can observe how to complete the logic elimination grid.

4. Give students a copy of *Hide 'N Seek*. This may be very difficult for some students. As the class works through the puzzle, it is important to observe students to determine which are able to quickly and correctly solve the puzzle on their own. For students who need more guidance, finish the puzzle together as guided practice. *Contest Conundrum* may also be used in class.

ANSWER KEY

Hide 'N Seek	*Contest Conundrum*
Max - bedroom	Prettiest - pecan
Jordan - kitchen	Sweetest - chocolate cream
Yolanda - under porch	Juiciest - peach
Isabel - tree	Tastiest - blueberry

CHALLENGE PAGES

Dudley's Daily Schedule *The Missing Biscuit*

5. Distribute the challenge pages to students. *Dudley's Daily Schedule* is a 4 x 4 logic grid which is the size students have been practicing on throughout this lesson. *The* Missing Biscuit is a 5 x 5 logic grid and may prove a little more challenging for students. To provide the best opportunity for diagnosing talented convergent learners, the challenge pages should be done individually.

ANSWER KEY

Dudley's Daily Schedule	*The Missing Biscuit*
9 AM - biscuit shop	Dudley - broken glass
10 AM - veterinarian	Max - the diary
11 AM - groomer	Sybil - the key
12 Noon - bookstore	Jordan - the lock
.....at the: bookstore	Dan - the paw print

DIAGNOSTIC NOTES

During this lesson, the teacher and observer will be looking for students who display specific characteristics. These students may then be invited to the small group sessions for additional activities. Some teachers explain the structure of the **PRIMARY EDUCATION THINKING SKILLS** curriculum to the students before actually starting the lessons. During the explanation, the teacher might point out to students the importance of volunteering during the lessons as this is the main opportunity for the teachers to observe what the students are thinking.

Characteristic behaviors and responses to look for are listed on the *PETS™ Behavioral Checklist - Convergent Thinking.* There is an overlap of characteristics between the units and certain traits will show up throughout the curriculum. The following is a short summary of what to look for in student behaviors and responses for Convergent Thinking, Whole Class Lesson 2:

GRASPS CONCEPTS QUICKLY - Look for students who quickly understand and use the process of logical elimination. List the students who are the first to figure out the correct answers.

SEES INTERRELATIONSHIP OF CLUES - Note students who combine information from various clues in order to determine the correct solution.

RECOGNIZES FLAWED REASONING - Look for students who point out errors in logic.

DEFERS JUDGMENT - Note students who wait until they have gathered enough information to figure out the correct answer. These students avoid guessing impulsively.

SEES ANSWERS INTUITIVELY - Some students who are excellent deductive thinkers are unable to verbalize how they figured out the answer. Note students who arrive at the correct conclusions without seeming to use the intermediate steps.

IS TENACIOUS - In addition to working diligently to the end of the activities, look for students who want to work on convergent-style activities. An enthusiasm towards this type of problem often indicates an ability to solve the problems.

RETAINS INFORMATION – When reviewing ideas from earlier lessons, look for students who clearly recall the concepts and then effectively apply them to the current lesson's activities. While many children may grasp concepts "in the moment" of the instructional lesson, these students exhibit the significant ability to retain and apply new learning across time.

Dinner Dilemma/Cuddly Creatures Club, Waffits & Zamboids, Perplexing Patterns 1, Perplexing Patterns 2, and ***Hidden Headgear***

Most important in the identification portion of this lesson will be those students who are able to complete these challenge pages correctly and independently. Note students who correctly solve the variety of puzzles. If a student has a specific strength in one type of puzzle, note that as well.

Dudley's Daily Schedule and ***The Missing Biscuit***

Most important in the identification portion of this lesson will be those students who complete these challenge pages correctly and independently. Note these students in the appropriate box at the bottom of the *PETS™ Behavioral Checklist - Convergent Thinking*.

NOTES

Dudley's Baffling Books

Early one rainy Thursday morning, Dudley the Detective's phone rang loudly, interrupting his daily duel with the crossword puzzle in the morning paper. On the other end of the line was Dudley's good friend, Sybil the Scientist, another logical, convergent thinker. Like Dudley, Sybil loves to create as well as solve challenging puzzles. However, on this particular morning, Sybil only wanted to borrow a book.

"No problem," Dudley replied, "but first you must tell me just where that mystery story sits in the line of books on my shelf."

"How in the world would I know that?" Sybil exclaimed. "You know I can't see your bookshelf! You're all the way across Crystal Pond Woods and it's too rainy to come over just now. Won't you just bring the book to me at the campfire tomorrow night?"

"Only after you solve this puzzle," Dudley insisted. He loves logic puzzles so much he makes them up whenever he can. "I'll give you some good clues that will help you solve for the right answer."

"All right," Sybil responded slowly, "but shouldn't I organize the clues to make them usable? I know that's an important step in convergent thinking. Should I use one of your famous **logic elimination grids**?"

Dudley smiled into the telephone. "Yes, it's simple to make one," he assured his friend. "Or as that great detective in the book you want to borrow would say, 'It's elementary.' Get a pencil and draw a square on a piece of paper." Dudley waited patiently while Sybil did this.

*(Project **Dudley's Baffling Books Logic Elimination Grid.** Cover all the clues until they are mentioned in the story. Solicit student responses as much as possible. Telling rather than reading the rest of the story may take less time.)*

"Now, there are four books on my shelf," Dudley said. "Into how many rows and columns will you divide your square?"

"Four," Sybil replied promptly, carefully dividing her square into four rows and four columns so it looked like a checkerboard or grid.

"Good thinking, my friend," encouraged Dudley. "Now, you might be surprised to find out that not all of my books are mysteries. In fact, the book you want is the only mystery on this shelf. There's a puzzle book, a book about bones, and an atlas that shows all the trees in Crystal Pond Woods. How can you use this information?"

"Those would make the labels for my rows. I should label one row **mystery**, one **puzzle**, one **bones**, and one **atlas**."

(Label the grid accordingly.)

"So far, so good," Dudley commended Sybil. "Now, what should you label your columns?"

"Well, since you told me I would have to figure out where the mystery book sits on the shelf, I suppose they should be called **first**, **second**, **third**, and **fourth**."

(Label the grid accordingly.)

"Indeed!" cried Dudley, beginning to sound very much like Sherlock Holmes. "Now for the clues, Sybil. The book of puzzles is first on the shelf."

"That means I should line up the row for **puzzle** with the column for **first** and find the cell in which they meet on the grid," Sybil said.

"Right you are," answered Dudley. "What mark did you put in that cell?"

"Since that's where the book is," explained Sybil. "I marked an **O** in that cell to show that I've found a match."

*(Place an **O** in cell 5.)*

"Super!" shouted Dudley. "Don't forget to make some elimination marks as well."

"Oh, that's right! Since I know that no other book could be first on the shelf, I'll mark an **X** in all the other cells of the first column. Also, the puzzle book can't be anywhere else on the shelf either, so I'll mark out all the rest of the **puzzle** row with **X**'s in the cells."

*(Place **X**'s in cells 1, 9, 13, 6, 7, and 8.)*

Dudley grinned broadly, imagining his friend having so much fun with his puzzle. "Here's the next clue: The book on **bones** is between the **mystery** story and the **atlas**."

"What does that mean?" Sybil was sounding a bit perplexed. "I know the **puzzle** book is **first**, but I don't know where the **atlas** or the **mystery** is, so how can I tell where the **bone** book is?"

Dudley replied, "It's true you can't tell where it is, but if you're a good detective, you will know where it is **NOT**, and that's important information, too."

"Oh, I see!" Sybil cried proudly. "If the **bone** book is between the other two you mentioned, it can't be next to the **puzzle** book at all! It can't be **second** on the shelf! I should make an **X** there."

*(Place an **X** in cell 10.)*

"Good work," Dudley encouraged. "Keep going."

"There's more? Oh, yes! It can't be last on the shelf either, since that wouldn't be between two other books! I'll make an **X** where **bone** lines up with **fourth**, too."

*(Place an **X** in cell 12.)*

"Well, now, if the **bone** book isn't **first**, **second**, or **fourth**, it must be **third**."

"Great detective thinking!" Dudley was proud of his friend. "Now you have lots of marking to do."

"Yes, I do. I have to mark an **O** to show that the **bone** book is **third**, then mark out all other books for **third** on the shelf with **X**'s."

*(Place an **O** in cell 11 and place **X**'s in cells 3 and 15.)*

"What's my next clue, Dudley?" Sybil asked eagerly.

"One more clue should do it." Dudley thought for a really good one. "Here it is: the **atlas** is in between the **puzzle** book and the book on **bones**."

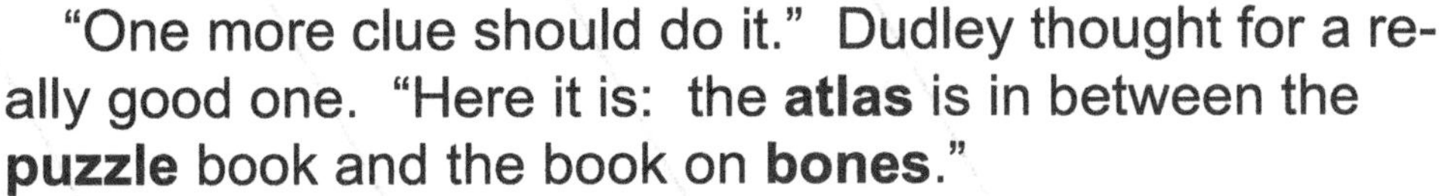

Sybil barely let Dudley finish the clue. "So I'll mark an **O** here to show that the **atlas** is **second** on the shelf and mark **X**'s in these two cells to complete this row and this column..."

*(Place an **O** in cell 14 and place **X**'s in cells 2 and 16.)*

"Oh! Look at this! Now I know! The **mystery** book I want to read must be **fourth** on your shelf!"

*(Place the final **O** in cell 4.)*

"Excellent detective work, Sybil!" congratulated Dudley. "I'll be sure to bring this book to you at tomorrow night's campfire."

"Thanks, Dudley, but don't bother now," replied Sybil. "The sun has come out, and it's no longer raining, so I think I'll just come over to your place right now, pick up the book, and then we can work on some more puzzles, OK?"

Dudley's Baffling Books

Logic Elimination Grid

	1	2	3	4
	5	6	7	8
	9	10	11	12
	13	14	15	16

1. The book of puzzles is first on the shelf.

2. The book on bones is between the mystery story and the atlas.

3. The atlas is between the puzzle book and the book on bones.

Name ______________________________

Hide 'N Seek

At Dudley the Detective's birthday party, four of his friends from Crystal Pond Woods decided to play hide 'n seek. Use this logic elimination grid to unravel the clues and find each of Dudley's friends as quickly as he did!

Visual thinker

Divergent thinker

Evaluative thinker

Divergent thinker

1. The four friends were Jordan the Judge, Max the Magician, Yolanda the Yarnspinner, and Isabel the Inventor.
2. The hiding places included in the bedroom, under the porch, in the kitchen, and behind the tree.
3. Jordan did not hide in the bedroom.
4. Isabel was not under the porch when Dudley went to look.
5. The friend in the kitchen was not a divergent thinker.
6. Isabel asked the friend under the porch if she could see Isabel's tail sticking out between the leaves.

Name ______________________________

Contest Conundrum

At the Crystal Celebration every summer, the pie-eating contest is a big favorite. Every prize-winning entry is always a special family recipe. This year, however, when Jordan the Judge placed ribbons on the winning pies, he got the ribbons all mixed up! NO pie has received the ribbon it should have. Use the clues below and the logic elimination grid to determine which pie really won which category in the contest.

1. The pies pictured have the wrong ribbons placed on them.
2. The peach pie does not have The Flakiest Crust.
3. The pecan pie was really voted The Prettiest Pie.
4. Neither the blueberry pie nor the chocolate cream pie won the ribbons that the apple pie and the pecan pie were given by mistake.

	The Flakiest Crust	The Juiciest Pie	The Tastiest Pie	The Prettiest Pie	The Sweetest Pie
pecan					
apple					
chocolate cream					
peach					
blueberry					

Name ______________________________

Dudley's Daily Schedule

Sybil the Scientist found Dudley the Detective's daily schedule book in Crystal Pond Woods. It was exactly noon. To return it to him, she needed to figure out where he was at this moment. Can you give her some help?

1. Dudley had four appointments in his book for that day: one at 9:00 AM, one at 10:00 AM, one at 11:00 AM, and one at noon.
2. The biscuit shop was the first appointment in the book.
3. The trip to the groomer was between the stop at the vet for some medicine and a trip to the bookstore.
4. Dudley would visit the veterinarian between his stop at the dog biscuit shop and the trip to the groomer.

	9:00 AM	10:00 AM	11:00 AM	12:00 Noon
biscuit shop				
groomer				
veterinarian				
bookstore				

Sybil found Dudley at the: ______________________.

Name ________________________________

The Missing Biscuit

Yolanda the Yarnspinner decided to spin a mystery yarn about a missing dog biscuit for Dudley the Detective to solve. Five friends from Crystal Pond Woods pitched in to help solve the mystery. The "sleuths" included Dudley, Max, Sybil, Jordan, and Dudley's cousin Dan. Each sleuth found one clue during the search. The clues included a paw print, a key, a broken lock on the biscuit box, a diary, and some broken glass. Use the logic elimination grid to determine which detective found which clue.

1. Neither Jordan nor Dudley's cousin found the broken glass.
2. At the time the broken lock was found, Dan and Max were searching around the stump of a tree for clues.
3. The one who found the key immediately ran to Dudley to show him what she had found.
4. The diary was discovered by Max in his own magic hat!

	a paw print	a key	a broken lock	a diary	broken glass
Dudley					
Max					
Sybil					
Jordan					
Dan					

CONVERGENT THINKING
WHOLE CLASS
LESSON 3

PURPOSE

The purpose of this lesson is to give students an opportunity to further develop their convergent thinking when playing a game which requires deductive logic and analytical thinking to arrive at the one correct solution.

MATERIALS

For projection:.
- *The Way to Convergent Thinking* signpost
- score sheet for *Aces, Jumble, Zilch*

For duplication:
- the story *Spot Check* to read aloud
- *PETS™ Behavioral Checklist - Convergent Thinking*

LESSON PLAN

1. Review with students the guidelines for convergent thinking using *The Way to Convergent Thinking* signpost:

- Find the clues.
- Read the clues.
- Take time and reflect.
- Organize and put the clues together.
- Determine the answer.

2. Read the story *Spot Check* aloud to students. The object of the game **Aces, Jumble, Zilch** is to correctly guess a three-digit number. These are the rules of the game:

- Students will determine three-digit numbers within a given range.
- Using the clues given after each number, marked by **AJZ** for **Aces, Jumble** or **Zilch**, the students will refine their three-digit numbers using deductive logic.
- **A** stands for **Ace**, which means the number has a correct digit in the correct location.
- **J** stands for **Jumble**, which means the number has a correct digit, but in the wrong place.
- **Z** stands for **Zilch**, which means the digit is entirely incorrect.

- **AJZ** should be used always in this order, regardless of the digit to which they actually refer, in order to increase the challenge of the game.

3. The game **Aces, Jumble, Zilch** can be difficult to visualize. The following is an example of how the game is played:

The Mystery Number is 634. The first number guessed is 164. The 4 digit is an **Ace** because it is the correct digit in the correct place. The teacher places an **A** after the three-digit number. The 6 is a **Jumble**, a correct digit but in the wrong place within the number. After the **A**, the teacher will write a **J**. The 1 is entirely an incorrect digit and earns a **Z**. To make this activity more challenging, all the **A**'s are listed first, then all the **J**'s, and finally all the **Z**'s earned by an individual guess, *regardless of the digits they represent*.

Using the **AJZ** clue, now the students suggest a second three-digit number. This time the number might be 145, assuming (incorrectly) that the 1 was the **Ace**, the 4 the **Jumble**, and the 6 the **Zilch**. The teacher should not comment on this guess, but respond by writing **JZZ** (**Jumble, Zilch, Zilch** for the 4,1,and 5 respectively.) The students must now combine this information with their previous clue to determine a new three-digit number. And the game continues.

4. While learning the game, it is easier if the Mystery Number is chosen within a specified range of numbers. It is also easier if the Mystery Number has no doubled digits. Therefore, if the teacher tells the students that the Mystery Number is between 100 and 300 (as it is in the story), the students can deduce that they really need to guess numbers between 102 and 298, reducing the range to allow for numbers with doubled digits. Here is how the responses to the guesses in the story will look:

127	AJZ
724	JZZ
265	JZZ
182	AAZ
172	AAZ
132	AAZ
102	AAA

In subsequent rounds, the range for the Mystery Number can be increased, perhaps to 100-500 or even 100-1000 (keeping the Mystery Number a three-digit number always), and the students can begin to guess numbers with doubled digits. When playing with the class as a whole, it is fun to set a specific number of clues in which the class must guess the Mystery Number. For instance, if the class figures out the Mystery Number in twelve clues or less, they win; if not, the teacher wins.

5. After completing the story, use the remainder of the class to play **Aces, Jumble, Zilch** with the students.

CHALLENGE PAGES

6. In place of a challenge page, incorporate playing the game as the challenge activity. Continue playing as a class throughout the year. Students can also play against each other, individually or in small groups.

DIAGNOSTIC NOTES

The following is a short summary of what to look for in student behaviors and responses for Convergent Thinking, Whole Class Lesson 3:

GRASPS CONCEPTS QUICKLY - Look for students who quickly understand the game and develop strategies for playing the game. Also note students who lead the game by selecting a Mystery Number and correctly giving clues in response to classmates' suggested numbers.

SEES INTERRELATIONSHIP OF CLUES - Note students who use previous clues to develop good guesses.

RECOGNIZES FLAWED REASONING - Some students will make guesses that do not make sense based on the clues. Look for students who notice those flaws in reasoning.

DEFERS JUDGMENT - Some students will wait until several clues are available before making a very valid guess. Even when the guess is incorrect, note these students.

SEES ANSWERS INTUITIVELY - Look for students who seem to make leaps in their patterns of guessing. This is different from impulsive random guessing because the guess is correct. These students may be unable to explain the guesses they do.

IS TENACIOUS - Look for students who want to play the game over and over. Also note students who stick to a game until they figure out the answer no matter how many steps it takes.

RETAINS INFORMATION – When reviewing ideas from earlier lessons, look for students who clearly recall the concepts and then effectively apply them to the current lesson's activities. While many children may grasp concepts "in the moment" of the instructional lesson, these students exhibit the significant ability to retain and apply new learning across time.

NOTES

Spot Check

The gamesters of Crystal Pond Woods were very excited. Dudley the Detective's cousin was coming to visit, all the way from the coast of the Adriatic Sea in Europe. Dudley had not seen his cousin Dan in many years, but he remembered that Dan was a spotted Dalmatian who loved to play games.

True to his word, Dudley introduced his cousin at the evening campfire to his friends. They were amazed by Dan's lovely, spotted coat. "How many black spots do you have on your coat?" Sybil the Scientist asked Dan, analyzing him carefully.

"Well, now," replied Dan, "figuring out the answer to that question would make an exciting game. You'll have to guess."

"But how will we ever know if our guesses are at all close? If we are thinking along the right lines?" queried Jordan the Judge.

"I'll give you clues," Dan replied.

"What kind of clues?" Dudley asked eagerly. "This sounds like a convergent thinking game! As you can see, Dan," Dudley pointed to ***The Way to Convergent Thinking*** signpost standing near the campfire, "important steps in convergent thinking are to **find** and then later **organize the clues**."

"Yes, I see," said Dan. "I call this game **Aces, Jumble, Zilch** and this is how it'll work... The first thing that you need to know is that the number of spots on my coat is a 3-digit number. It falls in between 100 and 300, and it has no duplicated digits in it. So you'll need to guess a number like that. I'll give you clues about your number in the form of an **A** or a **J** or a **Z**. **A** will stand for **Ace**. That'll mean that one of your digits is the correct digit in the correct place. **J** will stand for **Jumble**, which will mean that your number has a correct digit, but in the wrong place. And **Z** will stand for **Zilch**. That'll mean that a digit is completely incorrect."

"I see," said Yolanda the Yarnspinner, peering out of all eight lenses of her spectacles. "But isn't that awfully easy, since we'll see the three clue letters next to our 3-digit number?"

"No, because you won't know which digit each clue letter represents," replied Dan cryptically. "I'll give all the **Aces** clues first, then all the **Jumble** clues, and the **Zilch** clues last. That's how we'll **organize** your clues. In this game, it will be extremely important to follow your signpost and **reflect** on clues and **put clues together**."

"Cool!" Dudley exclaimed excitedly. "This sounds like a deductively good time! Let's try it!"

"OK," said Dan. "I'm thinking of the number of spots on my coat. Remember, it's a 3-digit number between 100 and 300, and it has no duplicated digits in it. Who wants to give the first guess?"

Sybil analyzed Dan's statement. "If there are no duplicated digits in your number, doesn't that really mean it falls between 102 and 298?"

"Good analytical thinking, Sybil!" complimented Dudley. "I think you are quite right! I'll guess 127."

*(Project the **Aces, Jumble, Zilch** score sheet to record numbers and clues.)*

Dan wrote **127** in the dirt outside the campfire where all could see it. After the number, he wrote his clue: **AJZ.**

"Let's see," Jordan stroked his chin feathers thoughtfully. "I believe that clue means that one of our digits is a correct digit in the correct place, one of our digits is the correct digit but in the wrong place, and one of our digits is completely incorrect. Am I understanding the clues properly?"

"Exactly right," Dan agreed. "The only hitch is that you don't know which digit each clue letter represents. That's where deductive logic will come in."

(At this point, the teacher may want to continue the game with the class, attempting to deduce the correct number of spots which is 102. As the

story continues, the class may reach a point where the game can be finished without the story.)

Rosalyn Robin was quick to chime in with a guess. "I'll guess **724**," she chirped. Dan drew **JZZ** in the dirt.

(*Ask students to explain what is wrong with Rosalyn's guess.*)

"Rosalyn," Jordan pointed out kindly, "Dan told us that the number had to fall within the 100-300 range. Your guess doesn't do that."

"That's true," Dudley agreed, as Rosalyn looked sheepish. "However, Rosalyn's guess isn't a total loss. It tells us that the 2 couldn't be the **Ace** from the first clue, because Rosalyn used a 2 in the middle of her number as well, and she doesn't have an **Ace** in her clue. Also, she moved the 7 from the end to the beginning. If it were the **Jumble** in the first clue, it may still be the **Jumble**, but it doesn't belong at the beginning or end of the number. Would you like to try again, Rosalyn?"

Rosalyn looked gratefully at Dudley. He had made her guess look smart instead of foolish. She tried to be less impulsive with her next number. "You have LOTS of spots," she said to Dan. "How about **265**?"

Dan drew **JZZ** in the dirt. He said nothing, but smiled slightly.

"This clue is important when you put it together with all the others!" exclaimed Dudley. "Look! If the number falls between 100-300 and it doesn't have any duplicated digits, it really falls between 102- 298. That means it has to begin with a 1 or a 2. You've put the 2 in the first spot in the number, but your clue doesn't have an **Ace** in it."

"So the correct answer has to begin with a 1!" exclaimed Rosalyn.

"That's right," agreed Dudley. "Now go back and look at our first number, 127. The **Ace** in that clue must stand for the 1. The **Jumble** must be the 2 or the 7."

"Plus," said Sybil, "if the 2 is the **Jumble**, it can't go at either the beginning OR the middle. See - - we've tried both those places and not received an **Ace** in our clue for it. That would mean the 2 would belong at the end."

"On the other hand," remarked Dudley, "if the **Jumble** stands for the 7, it would have to be the middle digit."

"Why?" asked Rosalyn.

(Ask students if anyone knows the answer to Rosalyn's question.)

"Well," Dudley responded, "7 can't be the first digit because then the number is too big for the correct range. And it can't be the last digit because the first clue only has one **Ace** in it, and we now know that stands for the 1."

"Wow!" said Rosalyn admiringly. "Now I know why you've become the best detective in the Woods."

"Next number?" called Dan.

"OK," said Sybil eagerly, "I think I can try again. I know I must begin with 1, and I should include a 2 or a 7, but not both. I also know I should not use 4."

"How do you know that?" asked Rosalyn now.

(Ask students if anyone knows the answer to Rosalyn's question.)

"The **Jumble** in the first clue stands for the 2 or the 7, right? The other one is a **Zilch**. The second clue uses a 4, but it only got one **Jumble**, and the other two were **Zilches**. That means the 4 is definitely a **Zilch**. I'll try **182**," concluded Sybil. Dan smiled broadly and wrote **AAZ** in the dirt.

"That's great!" exclaimed Dudley. "Either the 2 is now in the right place or the number should have 8 in the middle. We can test that out right now! I guess **172**."

"I thought we shouldn't use 7 and 2 together in the guess," said Rosalyn cautiously. She didn't want to seem to question Dudley's good idea.

"True," replied Dudley, "but this will tell us for sure whether the 2 or the 8 from the last clue earned the **Ace**." Dan drew **AAZ** again in the dirt.

"There you go!" Sybil smiled broadly. "You were right, Dudley. We now know that the 2 is in the right place, and all we have to do is figure out the correct middle digit. I've been analyzing this, and I realize we shouldn't use 4,5,6,7, or 8 because we've already used them in several places and they have always earned a **Zilch** response. That only leaves 3 or 9 since there are no repeated digits. I'll guess **132**."

Dan drew **AAZ** in the dirt again.

"Oh! Oh! The answer's 192!" blurted Rosalyn.

"Wait a minute," Jordan observed wisely. "Since Dudley would not want us to jump to any conclusions without all the facts, I must remind you that the middle digit might also be zero. When I look at Dan, I think he has closer to 100 spots than 200 spots, so I would like to guess **102**."

Dan quickly wrote **AAA** in the dirt. As the friends cheered, he complimented them for their excellent convergent thinking and suggested that now they try to guess how many trees were surrounding their campfire.

ACES, JUMBLE, ZILCH

ACE — a correct digit in the correct location
JUMBLE — a correct digit in the wrong location
ZILCH — an entirely incorrect digit

Number	AJZ			Number	AJZ		

CONVERGENT THINKING SMALL GROUP LESSON 1

PURPOSE

The purpose of the lesson is to introduce students to a more complex system of deductive logic using a double matrix logic elimination grid.

MATERIALS

For duplication:

- class set of *Logic Problem Planner 1*
- class set of *Logic Problem Planner 2*
- class set of *Soccer Rockers*
- class set of *Strategy Snacks*
- class set of *Crafty Critters*
- class set of *Jumpin' Jerseys*
- class set of *Election Celebration*
- *PETS™ Small Group Checklist* for each student

LESSON PLAN

1. As explained in the introduction, the *PETS™ Small Group Checklist* is used by the teachers to note additional behaviors that identify talented learners. A *PETS™ Small Group Checklist* is needed for each student in the small group lesson.

NOTE REGARDING SMALL GROUP LESSON 3

Small Group Lesson 3 is based on solving logic puzzles that students create. Give the assignment to create an original logic puzzle during this lesson so that students have time to prepare and bring the puzzles to the Small Group Lesson 2 meeting. This will allow the teacher time to look over the puzzles before using them in Small Group Lesson 3. Explain this to students and give each student a copy of *Logic Problem Planner 1* and *Logic Problem Planner 2*.

2. Introduce students to the concept of double matrix logic elimination grids by modeling *Soccer Rockers*. The following are the main points for solving double matrix logic elimination grids:

- Sometimes there is so much information that a double matrix logic elimination grid is needed.

- Each column and row is still labeled with information from the puzzle that will be used twice.
- O's and X's are used to show which information goes together and which information does not.
- After marking X's and O's for all the clues given, look within the double matrix grid for additional clues.

3. Students should work through the logic puzzles in the order given since the easier puzzles are first. Mancala is one of the games played in the puzzle *Strategy Snacks*. Mancala is an ancient African strategy game played with stones. Mancala boards and stones are available in most stores that sell games, and it is an excellent strategy game for students.

ANSWER KEY

Soccer Rockers
Sybil - Hornets - fullback
Dudley - Comets - goalkeeper
Isabel - Jets - forward

Crafty Critters
Yolanda - woodcarving - 1st place
Max - sketching - 2nd place
Jordan - painting - 4th place
Sybil - needlepoint - 3rd place

Election Celebration
Bill Johnson - President
Anna Smith - Vice-President
Wendy Jones - Treasurer
Matt Ferguson - Secretary

Strategy Snacks
Max - tic-tac-toe - doughnuts
Dudley - mancala - popcorn
Sybil - chess - brownies

Jumpin' Jerseys
Max - brown - 46"
Isabel - blue - 48"
Sybil - yellow - 45"
Dudley - black - 44"

DIAGNOSTIC NOTES

Note students who quickly understand and use the process of elimination. These will be the students who finish quickly and complete the grids correctly. Some students may intuitively solve the puzzles without seeming to go step by step through the grids. Note these students.

NOTES

Name ______________________________

Logic Problem Planner 1

Dudley the Detective wants you to create some logic problems to stump your classmates. To start off, try this:

1. Use these categories: math, recess, reading.
2. Make up the names of three friends.
3. Place the categories and names in the logic elimination grid.
4. Plan the problem you want to have solved. Write it in The Problem box.
5. Plan the answers you want.

The Problem

____
____
____
____
____
____
____

6. Write the clues for logically solving your problem. Use as few clues as possible.

a. ______________________________

b. ______________________________

c. ______________________________

d. ______________________________

e. ______________________________

Name ____________________

Logic Problem Planner 2

The Problem

____

____

____

____

____

____

This time Dudley the Detective wants you to create an original logic problem to stump your classmates totally on your own!

Use either 3 or 4 categories.

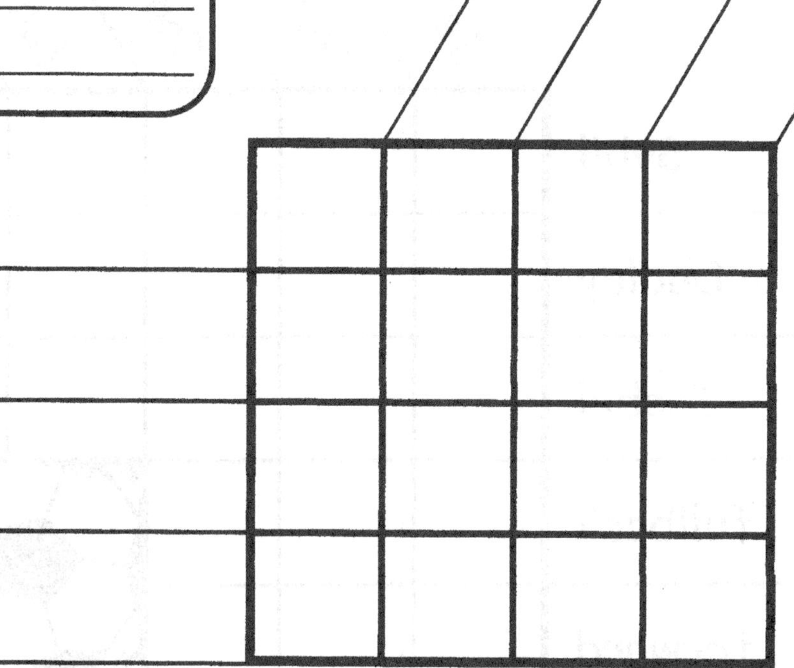

Clues

(Write as few as possible.)

a. ____________________

b. ____________________

c. ____________________

d. ____________________

e. ____________________

Name ______________________________________

Soccer Rockers

Sybil, Dudley, and Isabel play soccer for the Crystal Pond Park District. They each play for a different team and each of them plays a different position. Use the double matrix logic elimination grid to determine who plays what position and on which team!

	Jets	Hornets	Comets	fullback	forward	goalkeeper
Sybil						
Dudley						
Isabel						
fullback						
forward						
goalkeeper						

Clues

1. The fullback plays for the Hornets.

2. The goalkeeper knows his team beat the Jets last season.

3. Sybil plays the same position on her football team as she plays on her soccer team.

Name ______________________________

Strategy Snacks

Max, Dudley, and Sybil are members of the Strategy Game Club. They play board games that require thinking ahead to plan a winning strategy. When they meet, each brings a snack and a favorite game. Use this double matrix logic elimination grid to determine what game and snack each friend brought.

	mancala	tic-tac-toe	chess	popcorn	brownies	doughnuts
Max						
Dudley						
Sybil						
popcorn						
brownies						
doughnuts						

Clues

1. Some of the markers in Max's favorite strategy game are the same shape as his snack.

2. The chess player brought a treat that reminds her of her gameboard.

Name ______________________________

Crafty Critters

Yolanda, Max, Jordan, and Sybil won 1st, 2nd, 3rd, and 4th places at the Crystal Pond Arts & Crafts Competition. Use the clues below and the double matrix logic elimination grid to figure out what craft each friend entered in the contest and what place each won.

1. The friend entering the needlepoint scene of Crystal Pond Woods said she would have won a higher place if she had tied her knots more carefully.
2. Sybil won a higher place than her friend with the painting of Crystal Pond, but a lower place than Max.
3. Dudley told the woodcarver that he was proud of her good work.
4. Yolanda won a higher place than the charcoal sketcher.
5. Jordan did not win 3rd place.

	needlepoint	painting	woodcarving	sketching	1st place	2nd place	3rd place	4th place
Yolanda								
Max								
Jordan								
Sybil								
1st place								
2nd place								
3rd place								
4th place								

Name ______________________________

Jumpin' Jerseys

One afternoon, Max, Isabel, Sybil, and Dudley all participated in a long-jump contest at the annual Crystal Celebration. Each wore a differently colored jersey. The distances jumped included 44 inches, 45 inches, 46 inches, and 48 inches.

Guess who won! Use these clues and the double matrix logic elimination grid to figure it out

1. Max jumped two inches farther than the friend in the black jersey.
2. Neither Sybil nor Max jumped the farthest distance or the shortest distance.
3. Isabel wore blue, her favorite color.
4. The one wearing the brightest jersey achieved the only odd-numbered distance.

	blue	brown	black	yellow	44"	45"	46"	48"
Max								
Isabel								
Sybil								
Dudley								
44"								
45"								
46"								
48"								

Name ______________________________

Election Celebration

Dudley and Sybil were planning a party to celebrate the election of new officers for the Crystal Pond School Student Council. They invited all their friends from Crystal Pond Woods as well as the four new officers themselves. Unravel these clues to determine the full names of the new officers and what office each one holds on the student council.

1. Anna is the second in command to the president of the student council.
2. The four students include Matt, someone named Jones, Mr. and Mrs. Smith's daughter, and the president of the student council.
3. The Smith child plays on the same soccer team as the student council president and treasurer.
4. Wendy is good at math and keeps the accounts for the student council.
5. Mr. Johnson is proud that his son, Bill, serves as student council president.
6. The secretary of the student council is named Ferguson.
7. Anna's last name is Smith.

Treasurer
President
Vice-President
Secretary

CONVERGENT THINKING SMALL GROUP LESSON 2

PURPOSE

The purpose of this lesson is to provide students with an opportunity to use deductive logic in a format other than a matrix.

MATERIALS

For duplication:

- class set of *The Crystal Celebration Puzzle Pieces*
- class set of *1. The Crystal Celebration Parade*
- class set of *The Parade/The Costume Party* grids
- class set of *2. The Crystal Celebration Costume Party*
- class set of *3. The Crystal Celebration Car Race*
- class set of *The Car Race*
- class set of *Keeping Track*
- *PETS™ Small Group Checklist* for each student

LESSON PLAN

1. Prepare all the puzzle pieces for *The Crystal Celebration* before starting the activity. Laminate the character pieces, clues, and grids for use year after year. Store each separate set of puzzle pieces, grid, and clues in its own envelope.

NOTE REGARDING SMALL GROUP LESSON 3

Students should return *Logic Problem Planner 1* and *Logic Problem Planner 2*. This will allow the teacher time to read through the student puzzles before the Convergent Thinking, Small Group Lesson 3 meeting.

2. The Crystal Celebration puzzles are presented in order of difficulty. The first puzzle is fairly easy, and students will probably be able to complete it without needing much help. The second puzzle is a bit more challenging and is based on a clue from the first puzzle. The third puzzle is fairly difficult, and students may need to work in pairs or small groups in order to solve the puzzle.

3. Although these are manipulative logic puzzles, students may use any other strategies they have learned to help solve the puzzles. If students would like to attempt to use a logic grid, allow them to make one and try. It may not work as well as manipulating the character pieces, but the attempt to use previous knowledge should be noted on the *PETS™ Small Group Checklist*.

4. As students achieve varying levels of success with the different puzzles, *Keeping Track* allows them to monitor their progress. This formative assessment process is also helpful when these activities last longer than one class period to help students remember the puzzle on which they were working.

ANSWER KEY

1. The Crystal Celebration Parade

Jordan - fire engine
Yolanda - band float
Dudley - Garden Club float
Sybil - Science Club float
Isabel - Mayor's car
Max - clowns' float

2. The Crystal Celebration Costume Party

Jordan - cookies - cowboy - 6:20
Yolanda - cream pie - hula dancer - 6:10
Dudley - peanuts - elephant - 6:00
Sybil - cake - movie star - 6:15
Max - popcorn - clown - 6:20

3. The Crystal Celebration Car Race

1 - Yolanda - red
2 - Sybil - purple
3 - Dudley - blue
4 - Jordan - yellow
5 - Isabel - green
6 - Max - orange

DIAGNOSTIC NOTES

Look for students who complete the puzzles. Note those students who use several types of strategies. Note other students who seem to organize and structure all the clues mentally.

Jordan	Yolanda	Dudley	Sybil	Isabel	Max
fire engine	band float	Garden Club float	Science Club float	Mayor's car	clowns float

Crystal Celebration Parade Pieces ↑

The Crystal Celebration Puzzle Pieces

Crystal Celebration Costume Party Pieces →

cookies	cream pie	peanuts	cake	popcorn
cowboy costume	hula dancer costume	elephant costume	movie star costume	clown costume
6:20 pm	6:10 pm	6:00 pm	6:15 pm	6:20 pm

Crystal Celebration Car Race Pieces ↓

Yolanda	Sybil	Dudley	Jordan	Isabel	Max
red car	purple car	blue car	yellow car	green car	orange car

1. The Crystal Celebration Parade

Every summer, Crystal Pond Woods kicks off its annual Crystal Celebration with a big parade. Unravel the clues to determine the parade line-up of floats and vehicles. Place each character on the right conveyance.

The Crystal Celebration Parade Clues

1. Dudley did not lead the parade.
2. The float with the clowns brought up the rear of the parade.
3. Jordan sported a red hat to match the emergency vehicle on which he rode.
4. Yolanda rode the band float, playing 4 different percussion instruments.
5. The siren at the front of the parade warned everyone to get out of the way.
6. As the Science Club sponsor, Sybil rode their float proudly proudly, even though she was sorry not to be near the band.
7. Dudley was proud that his friend Isabel had been asked to ride in the Mayor's car.
8. Yolanda did not line up next to any of the other females.
9. No one recognized Max with his oversized shoes and rainbow curls.
10. Isabel was too far away from Dudley to talk to him, but she was right behind Sybil.

The Parade

	1	2	3	4	5	6
Animal						
Transport						

The Costume Party

	Jordan	Yolanda	Dudley	Sybil	Max
snack					
costume					
time					

2. The Crystal Celebration Costume Party

As part of the Crystal Celebration, Isabel invited Max, Dudley, Sybil, Jordan, and Yolanda to a costume party. The party began at 6:00 pm. Use the clues to match each friend with the correct costume worn, snack brought, and arrival time.

The Crystal Celebration Party Clues

1. Dudley arrived promptly at 6:00 pm, dressed as a circus animal with its favorite food.
2. Jordan's favorite treat was poppyseed cake, so he was very glad that Sybil had baked one.
3. Yolanda arrived 5 minutes before Sybil, wearing a costume suitable for dancing.
4. Jordan and Max arrived together, 10 minutes after Yolanda.
5. Max wore the same costume he had worn in the parade at the start of the Crystal Celebration . He did not, however, bring the chocolate cream pie.
6. The person who brought the popcorn did NOT dress as a cowboy.
7. Jordan's chocolate chip cookies were a big hit with his friend who dressed as a famous movie star.

3. The Crystal Celebration Car Race

One of the Crystal Celebration traditions is a car race. Dudley, Sybil, Isabel, Yolanda, Jordan, and Max entered cars in the race this year. Each car was a different color. Using the clues, place each friend in the right color car at the appropriate location on the race track.

The Crystal Celebration Car Race Clues

1. The two convergent thinkers raced neck and neck, but neither of them won the race nor drove a green car.
2. The orange car broke down before the first turn.
3. The driver of the green car had polished her fenders until they gleamed.
4. The yellow car traveled right behind Dudley, but ahead of Max and Isabel.
5. The red car finished in a spot that was not an even number.
6. Jordan was not in first or last place. Neither was the green car nor Sybil's purple car.
7. The victorious driver of the red car waved all eight legs as she crossed the finish line!

Which of these clue(s) are NOT needed to solve this puzzle? Why?

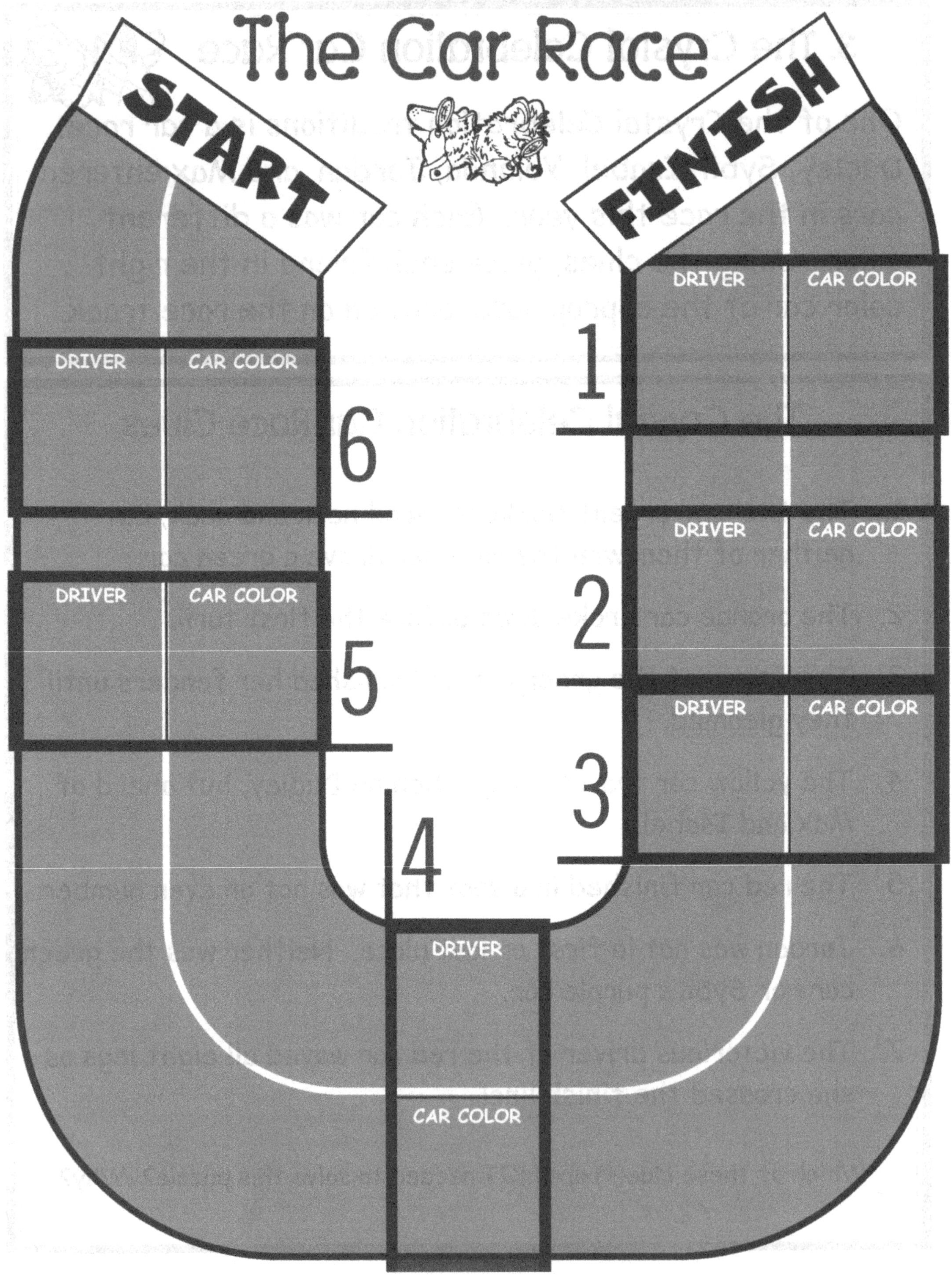
The Car Race
START
FINISH
DRIVER
CAR COLOR
1
DRIVER
CAR COLOR
2
DRIVER
CAR COLOR
3
DRIVER
CAR COLOR
4
DRIVER
CAR COLOR
5
DRIVER
CAR COLOR
6

Crystal Celebration: Keeping Track

Name:

	No chance to try this	Just out of the gate	Coming down the homestretch	Across the finish line!
Parade				
Costume Party				
Car Race				

Crystal Celebration: Keeping Track

Name:

	No chance to try this	Just out of the gate	Coming down the homestretch	Across the finish line!
Parade				
Costume Party				
Car Race				

CONVERGENT THINKING
SMALL GROUP
LESSON 3

PURPOSE

The purpose of this lesson is to allow students the opportunity to solve each other's logic puzzles and to discuss the characteristics that make a good logic puzzle.

MATERIALS

– the students' completed *Logic Planner 1* and *Logic Planner 2 distributed in Convergent Thinking, Small Group Lesson 1*

For duplication:

– class set of *Student Stumpers*
– *PETS™ Small Group Checklist* for each student

LESSON PLAN

1. During this lesson, students will attempt to solve each other's logic puzzles. Each student was to have completed *Logic Planner 1* and *Logic Planner 2* which were given to students in Convergent Thinking, Small Group Lesson 1. Give each student a copy of *Student Stumpers* to record their work and answers to the logic puzzles. All the grids on *Student Stumpers* are 4 x 4 grids. If some of the puzzles need a 3 x 3 grid, shade in the 4th row and 4th column to indicate they are not needed.

2. Begin by reading the student-created logic puzzle clues aloud. As each clue is read, have students write the appropriate labels and solve the puzzles on the *Student Stumpers* grid. Students' observations related to each puzzle's clues may provide diagnostic information as well as an opportunity for the teacher to direct the discussion. For example, if a puzzle's clues do not seem to work, the course of the discussion may revolve around how the clues could have been changed to make it a better logic puzzle.

3. Bring closure to the activity by discussing with students the characteristics that make a good logic puzzle. Possible questions to consider are:

What were the things they thought made a logic puzzle challenging?
Which clues were particularly creative and why?
Were too many clues given?
Which clues were not needed?
Were more clues needed?

DIAGNOSTIC NOTES

Note students who create interesting and subtle clues. Look for students whose puzzles were solvable but required that little bit of extra thinking. These students show the ability to understand the purpose of logic puzzles at a level above just being able to solve them. It is quite possible that none of the students in the small group will show these characteristics and that is okay.The group discussion may also provide insight into the thinking processes students used to create as well as solve the puzzles.

NOTES

Name ______________________________

Student Stumpers

Name

Name

Name

Name

Name

Name

Students are presented with the concepts of divergent thinking so necessary in many professions and a vital part of the problem-solving process so critical to the 21st century. Isabel the Inventor uses divergent thinking strategies as she invents. Yolanda the Yarnspinner uses divergent thinking strategies as she creates colorful stories. Students will learn the rules for brainstorming as well as the divergent thinking concepts of fluency, flexibility, originality, and elaboration.

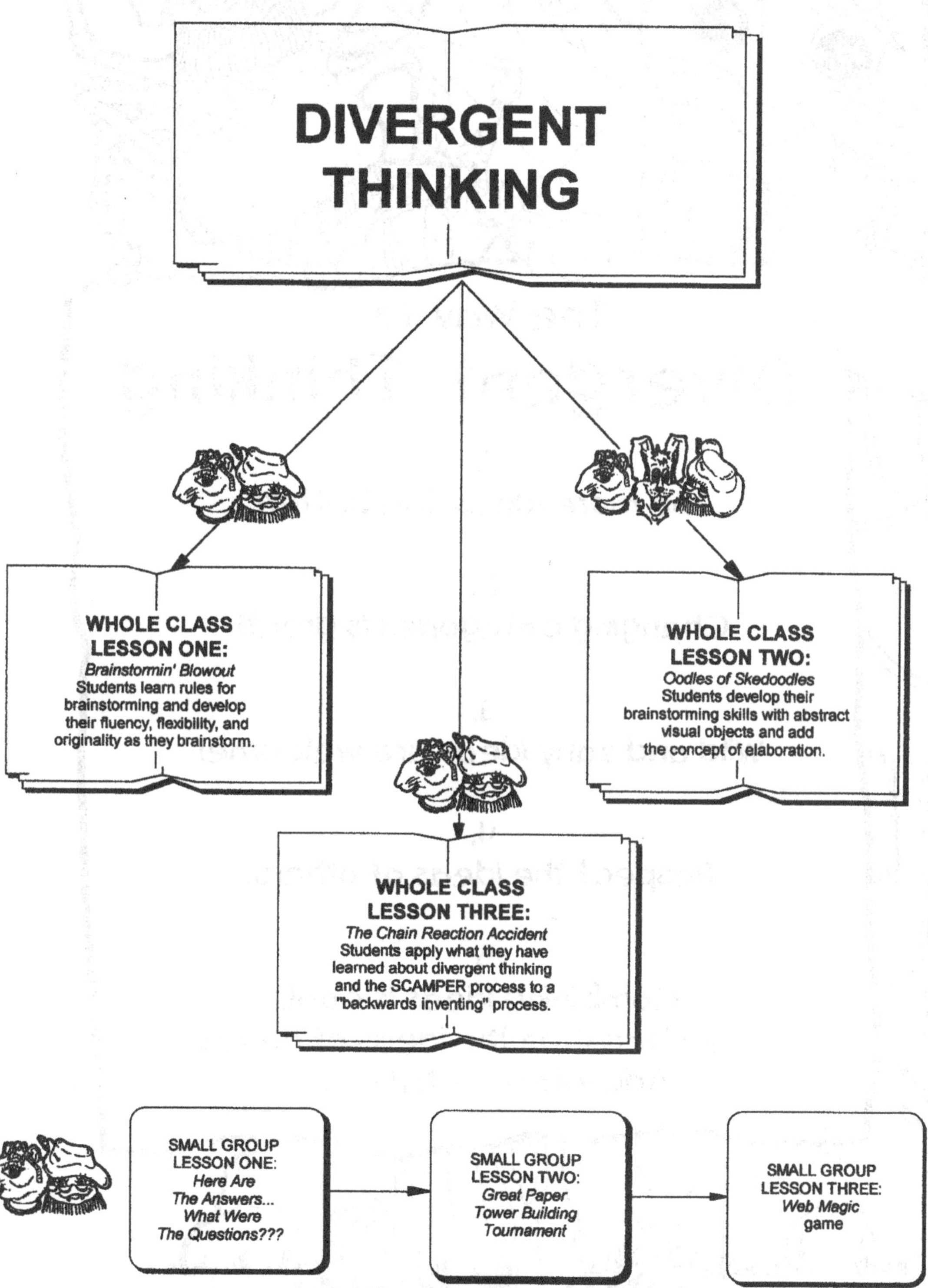

DIVERGENT THINKING

The Way to
Divergent Thinking
1.
The more ideas, the better!
2.
Changing categories is great!
3.
Wild and zany ideas are welcome!
4.
Respect the ideas of others.
5.
Combining ideas is cool.
"Piggyback" on the ideas of others.
Add lots of details, too!
merritt

List names of students as each behavior appears.

Add checkmarks after name if behavior is repeated.

Use a different color of ink or pencil for each whole group lesson.

PETS™

Behavioral Checklist

Divergent Thinking

(inventive/creative thinking)

Teacher
Grade ______

Dates of whole group instruction: 1. ________ 2. ________ 3. ________

OFFERS MANY IDEAS (fluency)	**CHANGES COURSE** OF IDEAS; SEES **DIFFERENT PERSPECTIVES** (flexibility)
OFFERS OFF-BEAT AND/OR **UNIQUE IDEAS;** WORKS OUTSIDE CONVENTIONAL PARAMETERS (originality)	**ADDS LOTS OF DETAILS** OR **EXPANDS ON AN IDEA** (elaboration)
DISPLAYS UNUSUAL OR **MATURE SENSE OF HUMOR**	**USES ADVANCED VOCABULARY** IN A MATURE, ARTICULATE MANNER
RETAINS INFORMATION FROM PREVIOUS LESSONS	**PETS™ CLASSWORK** INDICATES AN OUTSTANDING ABILITY TO USE THIS THINKING SKILL

I see these behaviors in these students regularly during class time as well:	These students did not stand out during the PETS™ lessons, but I see these behaviors during regular class time:	Notes:

DIAGNOSTIC NOTES • DIVERGENT THINKING

<table>
<tr>
<td>OFFERS MANY IDEAS (fluency)

♦ generates many ideas
♦ all responses are acceptable
♦ responses do not have to be creative</td>
<td>CHANGES COURSE OF IDEAS; SEES DIFFERENT PERSPECTIVES (flexibility)

♦ offers different types of responses
♦ changes categories
♦ sees things from different points of view</td>
</tr>
<tr>
<td>OFFERS OFF-BEAT AND/OR UNIQUE IDEAS; WORKS OUTSIDE CONVENTIONAL PARAMETERS (originality)

♦ shares ideas that are very different
♦ reponds in ways that "stop you in your tracks"</td>
<td>ADDS LOTS OF DETAILS OR EXPANDS ON AN IDEA (elaboration)

♦ spends a long time adding details that may not occur to others
♦ piggybacks on the ideas of others</td>
</tr>
<tr>
<td>DISPLAYS UNUSUAL OR MATURE SENSE OF HUMOR

♦ understands your jokes
♦ makes jokes you appreciate</td>
<td>USES ADVANCED VOCABULARY IN A MATURE, ARTICULATE MANNER

♦ correctly uses words others do not know
♦ expresses ideas in a more mature, articulate manner</td>
</tr>
<tr>
<td>RETAINS INFORMATION FROM PREVIOUS LESSONS

♦ shares knowledge accurately during review
♦ applies knowledge during activities</td>
<td>PETS™ CLASSWORK INDICATES AN OUTSTANDING ABILITY TO USE THIS THINKING SKILL

♦ seatwork and/or challenge papers are exceptionally well done</td>
</tr>
</table>

I see these behaviors in these students regularly during class time as well:	These students did not stand out during the PETS™ lessons, but I see these behaviors during regular class time:	Notes:
♦ *normally great divergent thinkers*	♦ *normally great divergent thinkers who "hid out" during the PETS™ lesson*	♦ *absentees* ♦ *new students*

- *be generous — more inclusive than exclusive*
- *names can go in more than one box per answer*
- *be sure to add ✓s after names for multiple answers*
- *be sure to use different colors for each whole group lesson*

DIVERGENT THINKING
WHOLE CLASS
LESSON 1

PURPOSE

The purpose of this lesson is to review the guidelines for divergent thinking and introduce the terms brainstorming, flexibility, fluency, and originality.

MATERIALS

For projection:
- *The Way to Divergent Thinking* signpost
- *Word Wiz: Fish*
- *Word Wiz*
- *Word Wiz Cards*

For duplication:
- the story *Brainstormin' Blowout* to read aloud
- class set of *Things That Go Up & Down*
- class set of *The Whatchamacallit*
- PETS™ *Behavioral Checklist - Divergent Thinking*

– a 3-minute egg timer (optional)

LESSON PLAN

1. Review with students the guidelines for convergent thinking. If students have completed **PRIMARY EDUCATION THINKING SKILLS 1** or **PRIMARY EDUCATION THINKING SKILLS 2**, they have learned about divergent thinking. The term divergent thinking was introduced and students were encouraged to branch off (diverge) and think of as many possibilities as possible. The guidelines for divergent thinking are listed below and on *The Way to Divergent Thinking* signpost. The term **divergent thinking** as well as the following guidelines are presented in the story *Brainstormin' Blowout*:

- The more ideas, the better!
- Starting new categories is great!
- Wild and zany ideas are welcome!
- Respect the ideas of others.
- Combining ideas is cool. "Piggyback" on the ideas of others. Add lots of details, too!

2. This lesson focuses on the brainstorming aspect of divergent thinking. Brainstorming has been introduced in the earlier books, but this lesson takes the concept of divergent

thinking a step further. In the story, a scoring system is presented to assess the brainstorming sessions. The scoring system may be used for almost any type of brainstorming. Points are given for fluency, flexibility, and originality. **Fluency** is the generation of many ideas or responses. Since the purpose of brainstorming is to have many ideas from which to choose when problem solving, be sure to accept every single response given. When scoring fluency, give each response one point. **Flexibility** is the ability to change the category of responses. In the story, the characters are brainstorming ways to use the word **fish**. Types of fish would be one category. The student who mentions fishing pole has started a new category of equipment and is showing flexibility of thought. When the brainstorming is finished, look for the various types of categories into which the responses fall and each type of category earns one point. **Originality** is the unexpected creative response and is therefore given three points. For example, FISHING FOR A COMPLIMENT may be a unique response earning 3 points.

3. Read the story *Brainstormin' Blowout* aloud to students. During the story, there will be an opportunity for class brainstorming. The three-minute time limit suggested in the story may be adjusted as needed. Sometimes students continue to come up with additional ideas that may be added to the list long after the brainstorming session has ended.

4. The *Word Wiz Cards* provide additional word stems to brainstorm. When using the cards, instruct students to use the word in as many ways as they can. Responses can be any form or derivative of the word on the card. Homophones are also acceptable as is any response given by students since brainstorming is nonjudgmental. The remainder of the class time can be spent choosing *Word Wiz Cards* to brainstorm and scoring the class lists. It is not necessary to do all the cards. More important is to brainstorm a card as thoroughly as possible. Usually in brainstorming there is a lull and some of the best ideas come after the lull. Allow students a chance to experience this.

CHALLENGE PAGES

Things That Go Up & Down
The Whatchamacallit

5. Distribute *Things That Go Up & Down* and *The Whatchamacallit*. Both challenge pages provide students with a different type of brainstorming opportunity.

DIAGNOSTIC NOTES

The following is a short summary of what to look for in the student behaviors and responses for Divergent Thinking, Whole Class Lesson 1:

OFFERS MANY IDEAS (fluency) - All responses are acceptable. Look for students who provide many ideas. These responses do not have to be creative.

CHANGES COURSE/SEES DIFFERENT PERSPECTIVES (flexibility) - This reflects a student's flexibility of thought. Note students who start new categories while brainstorming or show that they can consider a problem from different viewpoints.

OFFERS OFF-BEAT, UNIQUE IDEAS (originality) **-** Look for students with ideas that are very different. These are responses that may not occur to other students. They are the responses that "stop you in your tracks" and score originality points.

ADDS LOTS OF DETAILS OR EXPANDS ON AN IDEA (elaboration) - Note students who spend a long time adding details that may not occur to other students. Elaboration is more difficult to spot in this session but should be noted if it does occur.

DISPLAYS UNUSUAL OR MATURE SENSE OF HUMOR - Many talented learners have an advanced sense of humor. These divergent thinking activities provide opportunities for students to display this sense of humor.

USES ADVANCED VOCABULARY - Note the students who correctly use words other students their age may not know. They sound very adult in the way they express themselves.

RETAINS INFORMATION – When reviewing ideas from earlier lessons, look for students who clearly recall the concepts and then effectively apply them to the current lesson's activities. While many children may grasp concepts "in the moment" of the instructional lesson, these students exhibit the significant ability to retain and apply new learning across time.

Things That Go Up & Down and ***The Whatchamacallit***

The challenge pages do not include a scoring guide but may be scored if time and numbers allow using the same format as *Word Wiz*. The important thing is to look for students who show fluency and flexibility of thought as well as students with creative, original ideas.

NOTES

Brainstormin' Blowout

Isabel the Inventor was in the mood for one of her favorite activities and asked Yolanda the Yarnspinner to join her for a session of brainstorming. She knew that Yolanda, known for her love of colorful words, had recently created a new brainstorming word game!

"I can't wait to try out your new game, Yolanda. You know how much I love to brainstorm," Isabel announced as she joined Yolanda and their old friend, Max the Magician, in the meadow.

"Almost as much as I love games!" exclaimed Max.

Yolanda smiled proudly. "The name of my game is **Word Wiz**. It combines my love of words and Isabel's specialty, brainstorming. However, before I explain how to play the game, we need to make sure you understand what brainstorming is."

"Brainstorming. Sounds like a thunderstorm going on in your head," mused Max.

(Project ***The Way to Divergent Thinking*** *signpost. Cover the five guidelines, uncovering each one as it is presented in the story.)*

"Sort of," laughed Isabel. "Brainstorming is a type of **divergent thinking**. When you brainstorm, you try to get as many ideas as possible, like all the raindrops in a storm. The more ideas the better. Your brain has to work very fast."

"**Fluency** of thought," chimed in Yolanda, "is another way of describing thinking of many ideas."

(Uncover the first guideline and write ***fluency*** *next to it.)*

"And," continued Isabel, "you also want to push your brain to change course and see things in all kinds of different ways."

"Which is called **flexibility** of thought," Yolanda pointed out as she wrote that down, too.

(Uncover the second guideline and write ***flexibility*** *next to it.)*

"Wild and zany is also important when you're brainstorming." Isabel was on a roll now. "You want to think of unusual ideas no one else has considered. This is **originality**."

(Uncover the third guideline and write ***originality*** *next it.)*

"That brings up another important guideline in brainstorming," Isabel added thoughtfully. "All ideas are accepted. We need to be respectful and not judge another person's ideas as good or bad. And every idea is written down."

(Uncover the fourth and fifth guidelines.)

"This is very important," agreed Yolanda. "Even if I think of a silly, impossible idea, it might spark a really good creative idea from someone else. This piggybacking encourages some very creative ideas."

"Okay, okay." Max was getting impatient. "Now that I understand brainstorming - and fluency, flexibility, and originality - how do we play the game?!"

Yolanda held out a deck of **Word Wiz Cards**. "Pick a card," she instructed Max, who picked the word **fish**. "This is the starting point or the stem from which our ideas will flow. For three minutes we are going to brainstorm all the ways we can think of to use the word **fish**, and Isabel is going to write them all down."

*(Project **Word Wiz.** Give students an opportunity to brainstorm all the ways to use the word fish. Record their responses. Once the three minutes are up, stop and continue with the story.)*

Words had flown through the air as Isabel had frantically written ideas down, trying to keep up with all the ideas that were being generated. When the 3-minute timer had gone off, Isabel added the last idea. Now all three friends sat back to look at their work.

(Project ***Word Wiz: Fish.)***

"Wow!" sighed Max. "How challenging! We really thought of a lot of ideas. That represents fluency, doesn't it?"

"Yes," answered Yolanda. "And to score our brainstorming session, I'm going to give us a point for each answer on our list. That is our fluency score."

*(Record **15** in the fluency box. Project the student responses and determine the fluency score.)*

"We also get a point each time that we showed flexibility by changing a category."

Isabel had been pondering the responses. "I think I see seven different categories. We have ideas that are related to equipment, some that are food, and others that are expressions or idioms. You know, things that we say."

Max added, “We also have responses that are types of fishing, names of fish, parts of a fish, and I would consider GO FISH to be a title.”

“My favorite response is **selfish**. Yolanda, that was a stroke of genius to use the word fish within another word that has nothing to do with fish,” announced Isabel as she added eight points to their score for flexibility.

*(Record **8** in the flexibility box. Score the student responses for flexibility.)*

“**Selfish** is a very unique response and each unique, original response earns three points,” continued Isabel.

“I also think that **fishing for a compliment** is very original. What other responses do you think are unique?” asked Yolanda.

(Have students determine the unique and original responses on both lists. Then fill in the originality scores.)

“Now we can add together our fluency, flexibility, and originality scores,” continued Yolanda, “to determine a total divergent thinking score.”

(Add the scores for the three categories to determine the Divergent Thinking Total.)

“This is fun!” exclaimed Max. “Can we play again?”

“Sure,” laughed Yolanda. “Pick another **Word Wiz Card** and let the brainstorming begin!”

Fluency (1 pt)	Flexibility (1 pt)	Originality (3 pts)

Divergent Thinking Total	

WORD WIZ

fish

fish stick
fishing rod
fly fishing
sailfish
fish & chips
fishing lure
fish tale
fish hook
fish fry
fish scale
Go Fish
fish tail
sounds fishy to me
fishing for a compliment
fishing derby
selfish

Fluency (1 pt)	Flexibility (1 pt)	Originality (3 pts)
Divergent Thinking Total		

WORD WIZ CARDS

circle	chip	bag
star	watch	ship
high	ring	space
rose	key	top
note	land	night
net	line	can

Name ____________________

Things That Go Up & Down

Help Isabel and Yolanda brainstorm things that go up and down.
List your ideas below.

a yo-yo

your weight

Name ______________________________

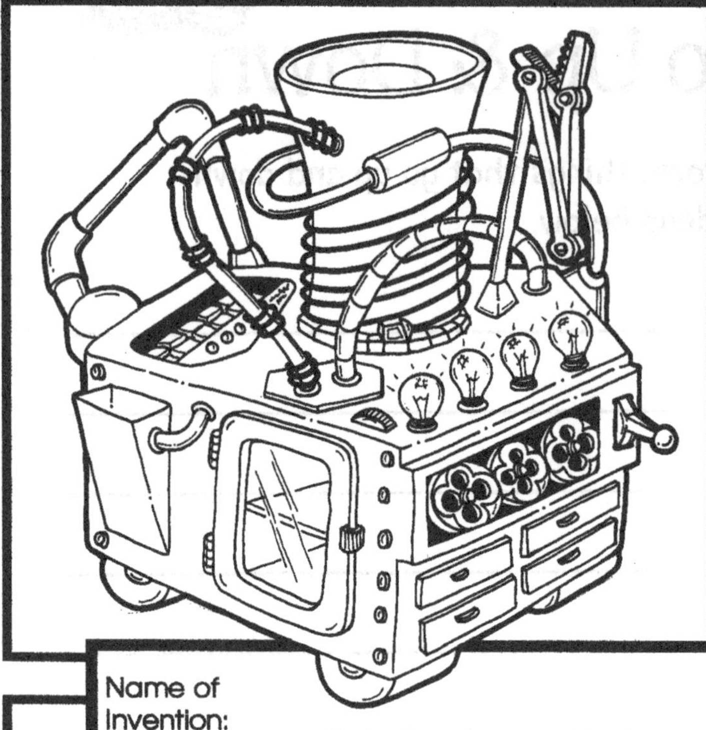

The Whatchamacallit

Isabel uses this wonderful new creation of hers to do many things at the same time!

Give this invention a name and help Yolanda tell about all that it can do!

Name of Invention:

DIVERGENT THINKING
WHOLE CLASS
LESSON 2

PURPOSE

The purpose of this lesson is to provide students the opportunity to brainstorm, emphasizing creativity, elaboration, and humor.

MATERIALS

For projection:
- *The Way to Divergent Thinking* signpost
- *Isabel's Creation* and *Max's Work*
- *Skedoodles 1*
- *Skedoodles 2*

For duplication:
- the story *Oodles of Skedoodles* to read aloud
- class set of *Cool Skedoodles*
- class set of *Your Own Skedoodles*
- PETS™ *Behavioral Checklist - Divergent Thinking*

– 3-minute timer and 1-minute timer

LESSON PLAN

1. Review with students the guidelines for divergent thinking using *The Way to Divergent Thinking* signpost:

- The more ideas, the better!
- Starting new categories is great!
- Wild and zany ideas are welcome!
- Respect the ideas of others.
- Combining ideas is cool. "Piggyback" on the ideas of others.Add lots of details, too!

Also review the terms brainstorming, fluency, flexibility, and originality.

2. Ask students to take a blank sheet of paper and draw twenty circles on one side of the paper. The circles need to be big enough to write a word inside. Instruct students to brainstorm **things that are round** and write them in the circles. Allow three minutes for this activity.

3. After the three minutes are up, have students do a fluency count and write the number of responses on a corner of their papers. Ask students if they found it challenging to get 20 ideas during the three minutes. Since most students will have found this a challenge, the next part of the activity shows the advantage of group brainstorming. Ask the class if it is possible, as a class, to brainstorm 20 responses in less than a minute. Then prove it is true by going around the room and asking each student to name one thing that is round. Discuss how listening to other's ideas may have helped develop new ideas. Discuss with students how group brainstorming can be faster and more effective.

4. Read the story *Oodles of Skedoodles* aloud to students. The story encourages elaboration and humor in the brainstorming responses.

5. After reading the story, have students brainstorm captions for selected pictures from *Skedoodles 1* and *Skedoodles 2*.

CHALLENGE PAGES

Cool Skedoodles
Your Own Skedoodles

6. Distribute the challenge pages to students. Although group brainstorming was part of the lesson, students should work on *Cool Skedoodles* and *Your Own Skedoodles* individually to provide a better assessment opportunity.

Students need to keep their own skedoodles simple and abstract. Pass out *Your Own Skedoodles* prior to the work time. Tell students they are going to create some skedoodles but you are going to tell them exactly what elements they can use – and they are not to add anything else at any time. Here is one example:

- In Box 1, create a skedoodle (or design) using **ONLY 5 straight lines.** They may be horizontal, vertical, diagonal, short, long, parallel, or crossed.
- In Box 2, create a skedoodle (or design) using **ONLY 2 lines and 2 shapes.** Lines may be straight or curved, long or short, parallel or crossed, vertical, horizontal, or diagonal. Consider any closed shape – circle, square, triangle, etc.
- In Box 3, create a skedoodle (or design) using **ONLY 3 shapes.** Use any closed shape – circle, square, triangle, rectangle, hexagon, etc.
- In Box 4, create a skedoodle (or design) using **ONLY 4 lines.** they may be straight or curved, long or short, parallel or crossed, vertical, horizontal, or diagonal.

Allow students only a minute or two to create each skedoodle – keep it quick and simple. Collect and put these papers aside after the skedoodles are done until a later time when students will add only the captions. A variation of this is to allow students to caption other students' skeddodles.

DIAGNOSTIC NOTES

The following is a short summary of what to look for in the student behaviors and responses for Divergent Thinking, Whole Class Lesson 2:

OFFERS MANY IDEAS (fluency) - All responses are acceptable. Look for students who provide many ideas. These responses do not have to be creative.

CHANGES COURSE/SEES DIFFERENT PERSPECTIVES (flexibility) - This reflects a student's flexibility of thought. Note students who show that hey can consider a problem from different viewpoints.

OFFERS OFF-BEAT, UNIQUE IDEAS (originality) **-** Look for students with ideas that are very different. These are responses that may not occur to other students. They are the responses that "stop you in your tracks."

ADDS LOTS OF DETAILS OR EXPANDS ON AN IDEA (elaboration) - Note students who embellish their captions with lots of details that may not occur to other students.

DISPLAYS UNUSUAL OR MATURE SENSE OF HUMOR - Many talented learners have an advanced sense of humor. These divergent thinking activities provide opportunities for students to display this sense of humor.

USES ADVANCED VOCABULARY - Note the students who correctly use words other students their age may not know. They sound very adult in the way they express themselves.

RETAINS INFORMATION – When reviewing ideas from earlier lessons, look for students who clearly recall the concepts and then effectively apply them to the current lesson's activities. While many children may grasp concepts "in the moment" of the instructional lesson, these students exhibit the significant ability to retain and apply new learning across time.

Cool Skedoodles and ***Your Own Skedoodles***

Look for students who complete the activities and show unique and original ideas. Any student responses that bring about a chuckle or laugh have obviously shown an unusual or mature sense of humor. Note students who display detail or elaboration in their captions.

Oodles of Skedoodles

One lazy, sunny afternoon, Isabel the Inventor and Max the Magician were lying beside Crystal Pond, very near **The Way to Divergent Thinking** signpost. The friends were just doodling away with sticks in the soft, damp ground. Max looked over at Isabel's recent creation.

*(Project **Isabel's Creation.)***

"What's that you've drawn?" Max asked. "It looks sort of like a hand waving from under the water."

Isabel laughed. "I suppose it does," she agreed, "even though I had meant for it to look like a rooster walking behind a wall."

"Huh? Oh, sure! I can see that!" Max chuckled. "All that's showing is the top of the rooster's comb, right?"

Isabel smiled. "That's right, Max. Now let me see what you've drawn."

Max smiled back at his friend. "You know, the fun thing about this is that you don't have to be a great artist to join in. See what I mean?" Max pointed to his work.

*(Project **Max's Work**.)*

Isabel peered at Max's drawing. "A box?"

"Could be," agreed Max, "but remember what **The Way to Divergent Thinking** signpost tells us about being flexible thinkers and seeing things in all kinds of new and different ways? If this isn't just a box, what else could it be?"

"How about an apartment complex for rodents? With rooms sized to fit small mice, medium hamsters, and very large rats!" Isabel giggled, then gasped as Yolanda the Yarnspinner chose just that moment to drop down from the tree above and join her friends.

"That was such a lovely, elaborative answer, Isabel," complimented Yolanda. "I just LOVE a good detailed description or caption that uses interesting and colorful words to capture our imaginations. When you add lots and lots of details like that, did you know it's called **elaboration**?

*(Project **The Way to Divergent Thinking** signpost. Write **elaboration** by the fifth guideline.)*

"Elaboration is an important part of divergent thinking, just as fluency, flexibility, and originality are important. Elaborative captions are really the best, if you ask me. Now, Max, what did *you* plan this to be?"

*(Project **Max's Work** again.)*

Max grinned. "It's a cow who's been in a very small shed for far too long!" Isabel and Yolanda both burst out laughing.

"That's certainly unique. What an original idea, Max," said Isabel, catching her breath.

"Absolutely," agreed Yolanda. "This one idea of Max's shows **flexibility** (it's a very different way of looking at this drawing), **elaboration** (he added descriptive details), and **originality** (it's an idea I know I hadn't heard before). On top of all that, it even made me laugh!"

As the merriment finally subsided, Yolanda asked her friends, "So what do you call these fabulously flexible visual creations and their elaborative, creative captions? You must have just the right name for them, you know."

"Sketches!"

"Doodles!"

Both Max and Isabel answered at exactly the same time.

"Skedoodles!" proclaimed Yolanda. "How perfect! I LOVE it!"

As Yolanda was drooling over this enchanting new word for her word bank, Max was considering something else. "Hey, guys, we've also learned that fluency of ideas is important, too. Do you think we could come up with some more ideas for our two skedoodles?"

(Have students brainstorm other ideas for the two skedoodles. Encourage elaboration as well as flexibility, originality, and humor.)

"How about drawing more of these cool skedoodles?" suggested Isabel. "Divergent thinking can sure be fun!"

Max drew another shape in the dirt. "OK. How about this one? How would you describe or caption it?"

*(As a class, brainstorm descriptions/captions for **Skedoodles 1** and **Skedoodles 2**.)*

Isabel's Creation

Max's Work

Skedoodles 1

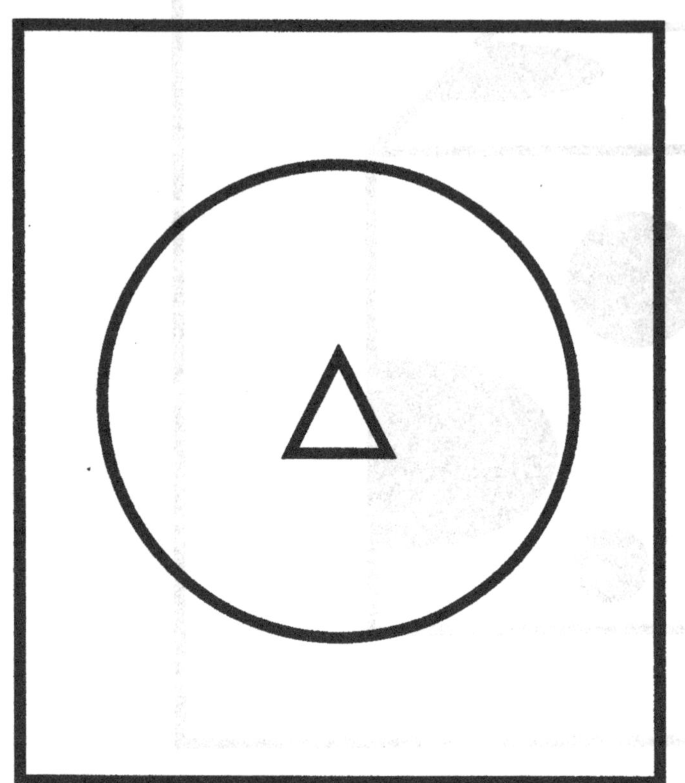

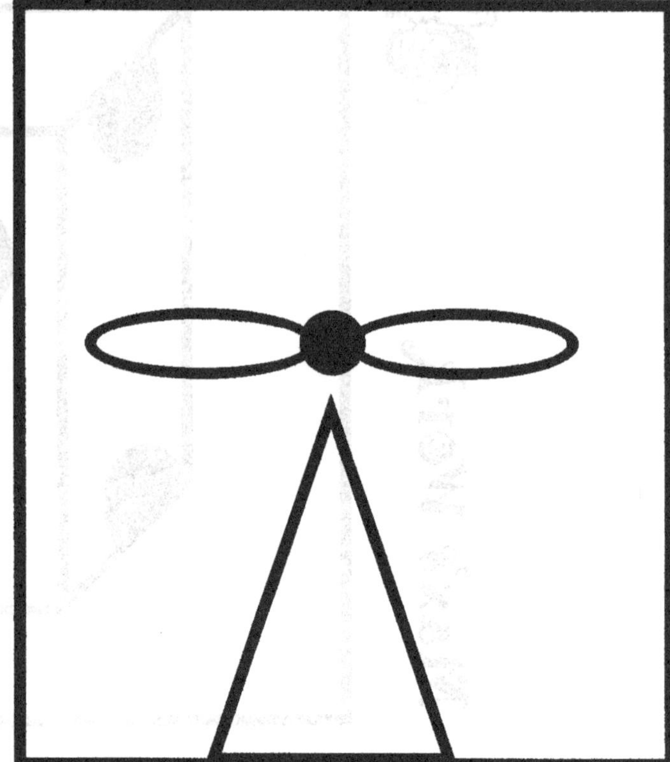

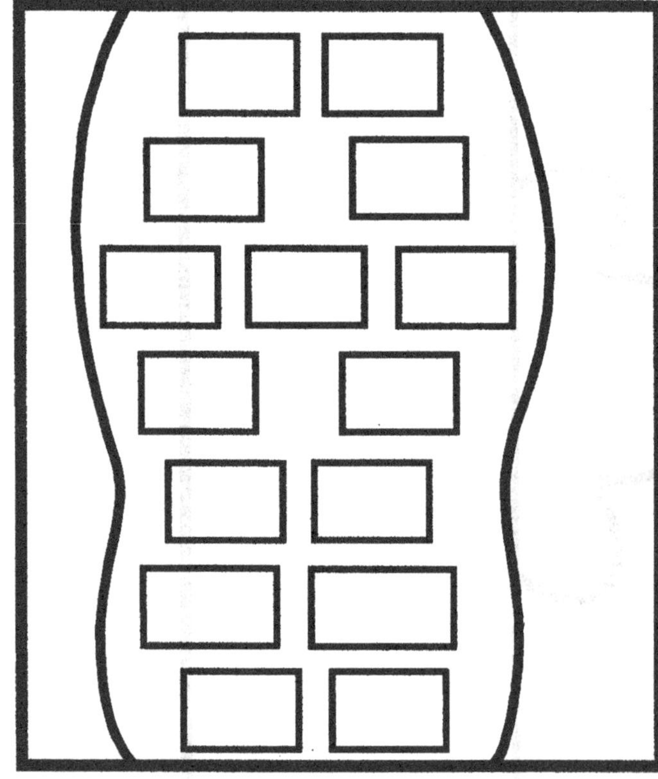

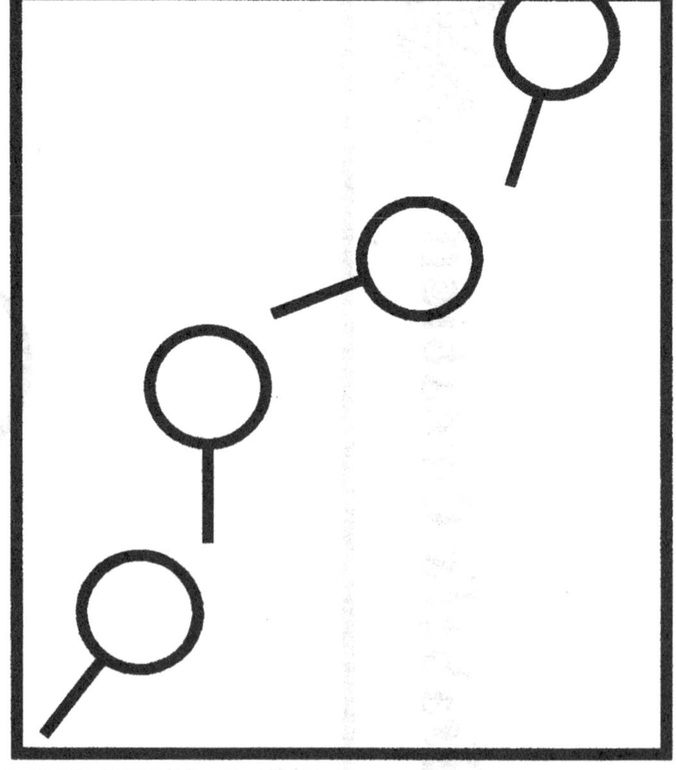

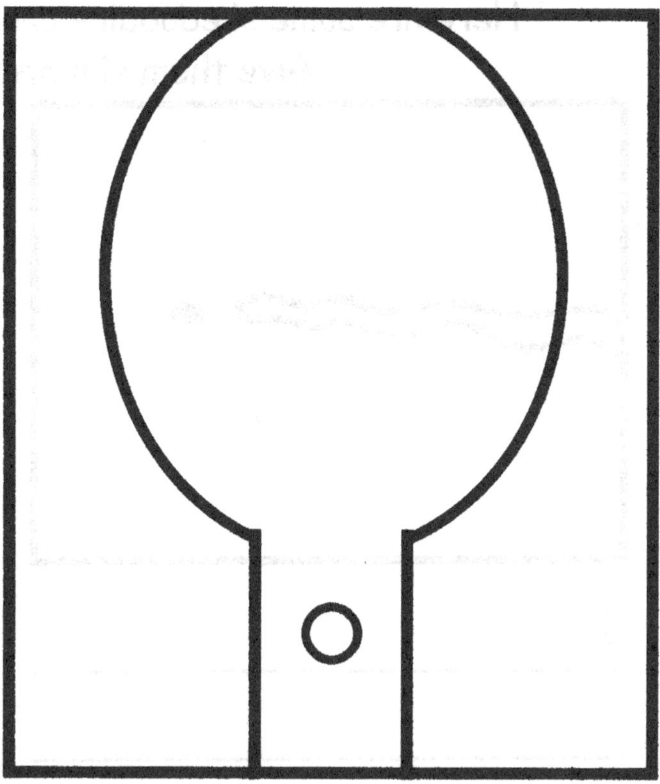

Name ______________________________

Cool Skedoodles

Here are some skedoodles created by friends of Isabel and Max.
Give them elaborative, creative captions.

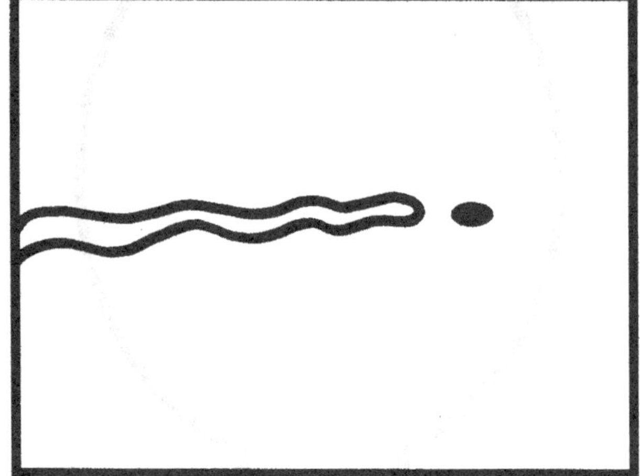

1. ______________________________

____

____

2. ______________________________

____

____

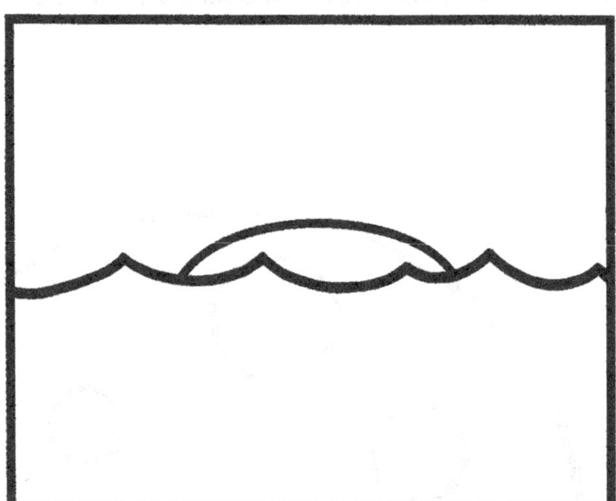

3. ______________________________

____

____

4. ______________________________

____

____

Name ______________________________

Your Own Skedoodles

Create your own skedoodles!
Give them elaborate, creative captions.

1. ______________________________

____

____

2. ______________________________

____

____

3. ______________________________

____

____

4. ______________________________

____

____

DIVERGENT THINKING WHOLE CLASS LESSON 3

PURPOSE

The purpose of this lesson is to give students the opportunity to use the inventive and elaborative aspects of divergent thinking.

MATERIALS

For projection:

- *The Way to Divergent Thinking* signpost
- *A Chain Reaction*
- *Max's Cool Contraption!*

For duplication:

- the story *The Chain Reaction Accident* to read aloud
- class set of *Pets, Parts, and Pieces*
- class set of *A Chain Reaction Contraption*
- *PETS™ Behavioral Checklist - Divergent Thinking*

LESSON PLAN

1. Review with students the guidelines for divergent thinking using *The Way to Divergent Thinking* signpost:

- The more ideas, the better!
- Starting new categories is great!
- Wild and zany ideas are welcome!
- Respect the ideas of others.
- Combining ideas is cool. "Piggyback" on the ideas of others. Add lots of details, too!

Also review the terms fluency, flexibility, originality, and elaboration.

2. If students have completed **PRIMARY EDUCATION THINKING SKILLS 1** or **PRIMARY EDUCATION THINKING SKILLS 2**, they learned about Isabel the Inventor who uses parts and pieces in unusual ways to solve problems. In addition, remind students that Yolanda the Yarnspinner's use of descriptive words greatly enhances the understanding and enjoyment of inventive thinking. The **SCAMPER** process was introduced to students in **PRIMARY EDUCATION THINKING SKILLS 2**. Although the type of inventing presented in this lesson is somewhat different than the **SCAMPER** process, reminding students of that process may be valuable.

SCAMPER stands for:

- **S**ubstitute something
- **C**ombine things
- **A**dd something
- **M**ake parts bigger or smaller
- **P**ut to another use
- **E**liminate something
- **R**earrange parts

3. The story *The Chain Reaction Accident* introduces students to Ruben Lucius Goldberg (1883 – 1970), an award-winning cartoonist commonly known as Rube Goldberg. Goldberg's cartoons are enjoyed for the improbable sequences or chains of events that accomplish a simple task in a very complex way. Intricate combinations of objects and animals interact to blow out birthday candles, swat a fly, wake you up in the morning, or walk the family dog. While each step alone may be possible, it is the improbable time frame (waiting for flowers to grow) or timing (a fish leaping at the right moment and direction) plus the ridiculous combination of steps that students will find fascinating. Goldberg used wheels, monkeys, pulleys, kites, and springs, all seemingly waiting in sequence to be tripped.

4. Read the story *The Chain Reaction Accident* aloud to students. Two examples of chain reaction contraptions are provided in the story.

5. Distribute *Pets, Parts, and Pieces* and *A Chain Reaction Contraption* to students. Have students invent a sequence of steps that accomplish the simple task of cracking open Isabel's acorns in an unnecessarily complicated and funny way. Students must use at least three of the objects from *Pets, Parts, and Pieces* along with anything else they would like to add. They may use pictures cut from magazines or simply draw the parts they need to develop an original *Chain Reaction Contraption*. Some students prefer only to draw, taking inspiration from the *Pets, Parts, and Pieces* page and their own imaginations. Sometimes it is helpful if students clarify the action in their cartoons by adding lines to indicate direction of movement: the flopping of a fish, the bounce of a ball, or the trajectory of a marble. Each step on its own should be fairly possible. It is the combination of steps that demonstrates the student's creativity and elaboration.

6. When drawing and pasting is completed, have students number and label the steps of their contraptions. Coax students to use words creatively as each student elaborates on his or her contraption in a separate descriptive paragraph.

7. Encourage students to work independently so that individual divergent thinking skills can be more accurately assessed.

CHALLENGE PAGE

A Chain Reaction Contraption

8. Completing *A Contraption Chain Reaction* is the challenge page for this lesson.

DIAGNOSTIC NOTES

The following is a short summary of what to look for in the student behaviors and responses for Divergent Thinking, Whole Class Lesson 3:

OFFERS MANY IDEAS (fluency) - All responses are acceptable. Look for students who provide many steps to their cartoons. These responses do not have to be creative.

CHANGES COURSE/SEES DIFFERENT PERSPECTIVES (flexibility) - Note students who show, by idea or word choice, that they can consider a concept in more than one way.

OFFERS OFF-BEAT, UNIQUE IDEAS (originality) - Look for students whose cartoons are very different and unique. Look for students whose words or phrases are not thought of by other students. These are the "off beat" ideas and responses that "stop you in your tracks."

ADDS LOTS OF DETAILS OR EXPANDS ON AN IDEA (elaboration) - Look for students who spend a long time adding details not thought of by other students. Note students who elaborate in the writing portion of the lesson.

DISPLAYS UNUSUAL OR MATURE SENSE OF HUMOR - Many talented learners have an advanced sense of humor. Look for students whose combination of cartoon steps and writing show a subtle or advanced sense of humor.

USES ADVANCED VOCABULARY - Look for students who understand the meanings of words beyond their grade level and use them correctly in their writing.

RETAINS INFORMATION – When reviewing ideas from earlier lessons, look for students who clearly recall the concepts and then effectively apply them to the current lesson's activities. While many children may grasp concepts "in the moment" of the instructional lesson, these students exhibit the significant ability to retain and apply new learning across time.

A Chain Reaction Contraption

Look for students who demonstrate an understanding of a chain reaction sequence of events by completing a workable invention. Note students who display humor and creativity. Elaboration is an important aspect of this lesson and should be noted. The use of colorful words should also be noted.

The Chain Reaction Accident

Isabel the Inventor loves inventing and believes anyone can invent. "Inventing is just idea-making," she said to no one in particular one day as she watched the goings-on in Crystal Pond Woods. She was perched way up in her old oak tree, directly above **The Way to Divergent Thinking** signpost. She saw her friend, Yolanda the Yarnspinner, carefully weaving an elaborate web near the edge of the pond. Fred Frog was sleeping soundly on a lily pad in the sun, while Max the Magician was designing a very intricate tower out of bricks in the clearing beneath her tree. She was about to call down to Max and warn him not to mix any of his bricks with her nearby stack of acorns when she spotted Dudley the Detective rushing up the path to the laboratory of his pal, Sybil the Scientist.

Dudley was struggling to carry something that was big, round, and black. As he climbed the steps to the lab, however, the door flew open and Sybil careened right into Dudley, knocking that black object out of his arms! It flew into the air, then rolled across the path right into the campfire log pile. CRASH! Logs went flying, cartwheeling and rolling everywhere! One log even bounced into the pond, scaring Fred Frog so much that he leaped up from his lily pad and crashed right through the new spider web that Yolanda had been spinning for hours!

"Wow!" exclaimed Isabel as she scampered down the tree and circled the clearing. After checking on her acorns, she hurried to the pond where a crowd was beginning to gather in response to this amazing "chain reaction accident."

(Be sure students understand what a "chain reaction" is.)

Meanwhile, Dudley and Sybil were trying to retrieve the black object, which had finally been identified as a bowling ball, from the underbrush, while Yolanda and the rest of the crowd were surveying her poor torn web.

"Fantastic!" exclaimed Isabel, as she joined the others. "What a great way to crack acorns!"

"What?!" demanded Dudley. Everyone stared at Isabel in amazement.

"Here - let me show you," Isabel offered, picking up a stick to draw in the dirt while she explained.

*(Project **A Chain Reaction.**)*

First Isabel pointed out how Dudley had rushed up the steps to Sybil's lab and collided with Sybil's door, causing the bowling ball to fly out of his hands and across the path, where it crashed into the log pile. The logs had exploded everywhere! One hit the pond with such a tremendous splash that Fred Frog was so seriously startled that he had leaped up and launched himself right through Yolanda's new web!

"Then," Isabel continued, "Fred landed in the wagon which I had been using to collect my acorns. The wagon with Fred in it then rolled down the hill and crashed into the tower of bricks that Max had built in the clearing under my tree! Fred's fine - I checked on him before coming over here. But the best part is that Max's tower of bricks fell on my acorn pile, cracking all the acorns for me!"

Everyone giggled and clapped, appreciating that a cool chain reaction contraption had resulted from this series of unfortunate accidents.

Then Max, who had been carefully studying Isabel's drawing, said, "You know, I've drawn a picture like this before. Wait right here while I go get it."

Max returned with his drawing. "I once learned about a famous cartoonist named Rube Goldberg. He liked to draw pictures of very, very complicated inventions that involved LOTS of steps and LOTS of details. He was very definitely into **elaboration**! However, the purpose of the invention was to accomplish only a very, very SIMPLE, routine task. I tried drawing my own crazy invention that is a series of chain reactions. Look at this!"

(Project ***Max's Cool Contraption!*** Discuss with students the steps involved in Max's contraption.)

"Why, how silly is that?" exclaimed Dudley. "Why wouldn't you just do the task in the easiest way possible?"

"Because, Dudley, it can be fun to try and do something easy in a new and unusual way," Isabel enthused. "Sometimes inventing is looking for an easier way to solve a problem, but at other times, inventing means seeing a different way of doing those ordinary, everyday, routine tasks. That's what I love about inventing! I never thought about having bricks, a frog, a log, and even a bowling ball all help solve the problem of cracking open my acorns!"

"Besides," croaked Fred, hopping up to the crowd, "that was fun! Let's do it again!" Everyone hooted and laughed.

"But," wondered Isabel, "is there another zany way of cracking open my acorns?"

The Crystal Pond Woods creatures were all intrigued by this new challenge and quickly went their separate ways, intent on designing their own chain reaction contraptions for cracking open Isabel's acorns. Everyone, that is, except for Yolanda who decided that the first thing she needed to do was to change the location of her web!

A Chain Reaction

Max's Cool Contraption!

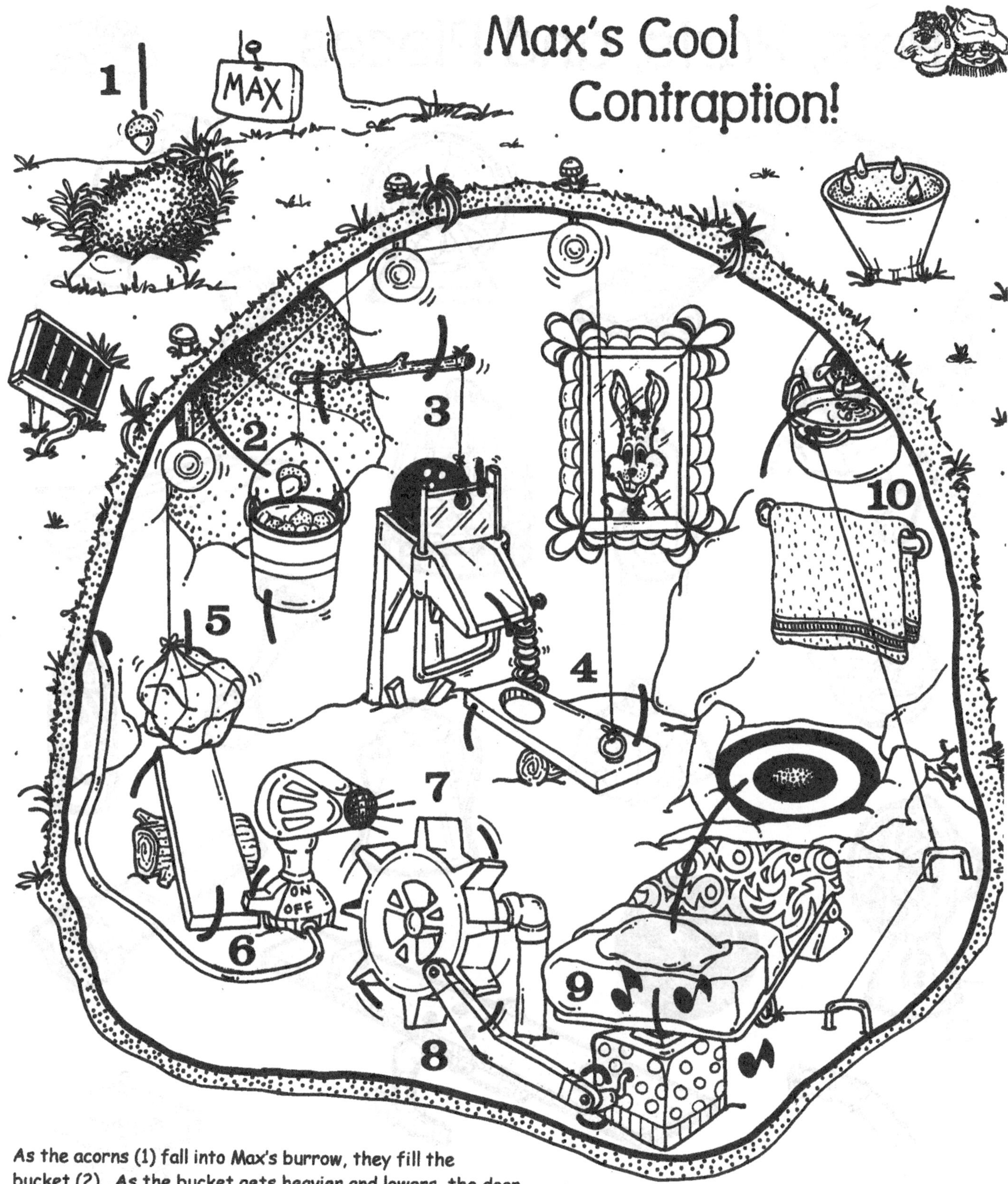

As the acorns (1) fall into Max's burrow, they fill the bucket (2). As the bucket gets heavier and lowers, the door on the chute (3) rises and releases the bowling ball. The ball falls on the lever (4), forcing the spring to stretch and the lever to lower. When the other end of the lever rises, the rock (5) is lowered onto a second lever which flicks up the switch on the hairdryer (6). The hairdryer (powered by the solar collector) blows air that turns the wheel (7) which turns the crank (8) attached to the handle of the jack-in-the- box. The jack-in-the-box plays, warning Max that it is about time to get up ... the box opens, flips up Max's bed (9), tossing him onto the target in the shower area and tipping the bucket of rainwater (10) that has been collecting. Max knows it is time to rise and shine!

Pets, Parts, and Pieces

100 LBS 100 LBS

COLA

A Chain Reaction Contraption

Create your own elaborate contraption to crack open Isabel's acorns.

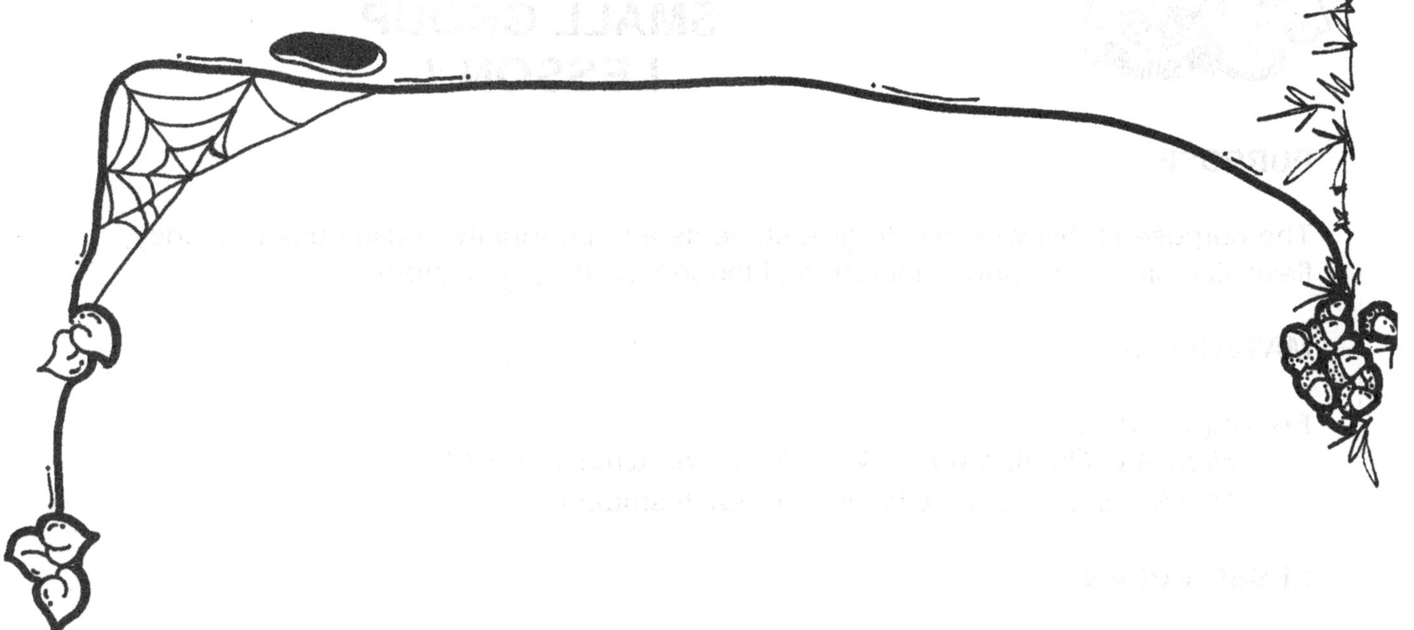

Inventor ______________________

DIVERGENT THINKING SMALL GROUP LESSON 1

PURPOSE

The purpose of this lesson is to give students an opportunity to use humor, fluency, flexibility, originality, and elaboration of thought as they brainstorm.

MATERIALS

For duplication:

– *Here Are The Answers...What Were The Questions???*
– *PETS™ Small Group Checklist* for each student

LESSON PLAN

1. Review with students the guidelines of divergent thinking:

- The more ideas, the better!
- Starting new categories is great!
- Wild and zany ideas are welcome!
- Respect the ideas of others..
- Combining ideas is cool. "Piggyback" on the ideas of others. Add lots of details, too!

2. Using *Here Are The Answers...What Were The Questions???*, read the first answer, "**Because it's so tall**," aloud to the group. Students are to think of what the question might have been to prompt such an answer. Since this is a small group setting, allow students to speak as they think of ideas rather than waiting to be called upon. This will facilitate the brainstorming process. As a student supplies a possible question, the teacher should only respond by repeating the answer.

For example, a student might say "Why does a giant have to duck to go through doorways?" The only reply necessary is "Because it's so tall." Other possible questions might be "Why does a tree sway in the wind?" or "Why do tourists flock to see the Sears Tower?" After each question, simply respond, "Because it's so tall." The students will hear if their questions have made sense. For example, "When do apples fall from the tree?" does not make sense followed by the response "Because it's so tall."

3. *Here Are The Answers...What Were The Questions???* lists answers in order of the difficulty to respond to. By starting with the easier answers, the students will have a chance to warm up before moving to the more difficult responses. This type of thinking seems backwards for them and is NOT easy!

4. It is not important to get through every answer. Allow each brainstorming session to wind down of its own accord giving students plenty of time to brainstorm all the ideas they can.

DIAGNOSTIC NOTES

Look for students who are fluent, flexible, and original thinkers. Elaboration is more difficult to spot in this session, but should be noted if it does occur. Fluent thinkers will be able to come up with many valid questions in response to the answers posed. Flexible thinkers will change categories in their ideas and will not simply repeat or minimally change the responses they have just heard from others or from themselves. Flexible thinkers will also be able to adjust to the new beginnings each question requires. For example, after listing questions beginning with "Why . . ." to go with "Because it's so tall," a flexible thinker will not be stumped by changing to "When" questions to respond to "After the stars come out." Original thinkers will look at the answer in a new way, giving it a twist that no one else thought of. For example, in response to the answer, "After the stars come out," an original, flexible response would be, "When's the best time to ask for an autograph?" Another example of an original response to "Over the first, under the second, and keep right on going" might be "What are the directions for weaving?"

NOTES

Here Are The Answers ... What Were The Questions???

Because it's so tall.
1

Every time the wind blows.
2

While it's still wet.
3

Anything that is soft.
4

After the stars come out.
5

Only if it is covered in peanut butter.
6

About 300 pounds and very angry.
7

Only when I sneeze.
8

Because the glue has not set yet.
9

Over the first, under the second, and keep right on going.
10

DIVERGENT THINKING
SMALL GROUP
LESSON 2

PURPOSE

The purpose of this lesson is to give students an opportunity to use divergent thinking skills in order to solve a problem.

MATERIALS

For duplication:

- *Awards for Isabel's Great Paper Tower Building Tourney*
- *PETS™ Small Group Checklist* for each student

- plenty of 8.5 x 11 white copying paper
- scissors for each group
- a roll of masking tape
- a meter stick

LESSON PLAN

1. Introduce the activity by asking students to brainstorm things which are very tall. Record student responses. Once the brainstorming session is completed, circle those responses which are tall buildings or towers. Ask students what kinds of things allow these tall buildings or towers to remain standing. The types of responses which will be helpful in the activity might include: a solid foundation, built with strong materials, use of supports sometimes in the shapes of triangles.

2. Divide students into pairs or triads to work on this activity. Explain to students that Isabel the Inventor is having a **Great Paper Tower Building Tournament**. The goal is to be the group with the tallest, free-standing tower. Contestants are to build a tower using one piece of 8.5 x 11 white sheet of paper and 15 cm of masking tape. A pair of scissors may also be used for cutting the paper but not as part of the tower.

3. As a group finishes building, the tower should be measured from the bottom to the highest point. The definition of free-standing can be determined by the group but is usually 15-30 seconds of standing without support. Record the height of the towers so students are aware of the tallest height so far.

4. Part of the inventing process is brainstorming and trying many different ideas. Allow students to start over with new materials, trying various types of structures as they attempt to beat the record. Encourage piggybacking as they see what others are doing.

5. Leave time at the end of the class to discuss what worked and what did not work. Also discuss what process of thinking students used in designing and testing towers and how divergent thinking played a role.

6. Use *Awards for Isabel's Great Paper Tower Building Tourney* to acknowledge those students with the tallest tower as well as those students who design a creative tower.

DIAGNOSTIC NOTES

Look for students who show fluency and flexibility in the design of their towers. Some students may get "stuck" and not see all the potential in one piece of paper. Other students will immediately have ideas or a vision of the structure before starting. Note those students. If students show elaboration or attention to details, record this type of divergent thinking. Note students who come up with original designs. Some students are more excited about building something creative rather than the tallest and those students who demonstrate exceptional creativity should be noted. Although all students will be able to build something, look for those students who show outstanding work by building the tallest tower.

NOTES

The Great Paper Tower Building
Tournament
The
Tallest
Tower

Awards
for
Isabel's
Great
Paper
Tower
Building
Tourney

The Great Paper Tower Building
Tournament
The
Tallest
Tower

The Great Paper Tower Building
Tournament
The Most
Creative
Tower

The Great Paper Tower Building
Tournament
The Most
Creative
Tower

DIVERGENT THINKING SMALL GROUP LESSON 3

PURPOSE

The purpose of this lesson is to give students further opportunity to develop their divergent thinking skills as they brainstorm word webs.

MATERIALS

For duplication:

- *Web Magic* score sheet
- *PETS™ Small Group Checklist* for each student

- clock or 10-minute timer
- chart or butcher paper
- markers

LESSON PLAN

1. Review with students the guidelines of divergent thinking. Students will be brainstorming but in a different way than they have in previous lessons.

2. Model the technique for brainstorming a word web and how to score it. The following example may be used:

Write the KEY WORD, **ocean**, in the center of the paper in a circle. With the students, brainstorm words that are related to the KEY WORD, **ocean**. Words related to **ocean** may include **shore, fish, mammals, shells, boats, people, tides, reef**, and **bottom.** Add these to the web as illustrated.

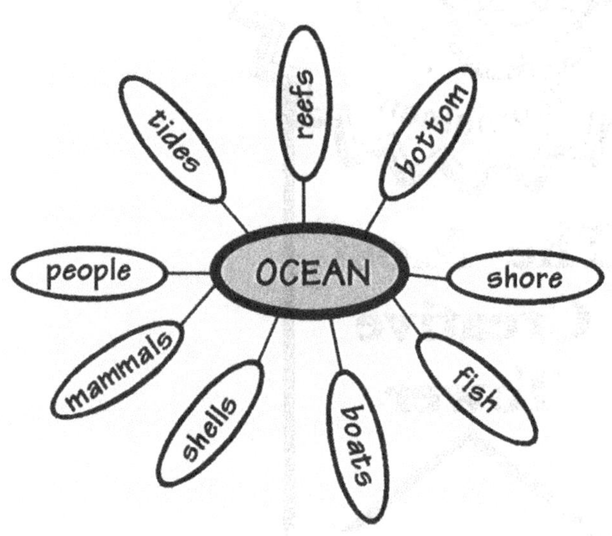

Continue the brainstorming with each of these words treated as a KEY WORD. For example, **boats** may have lines drawn from it including the following types of boats: **military, cargo, sail, cruise**, and **recreational**.

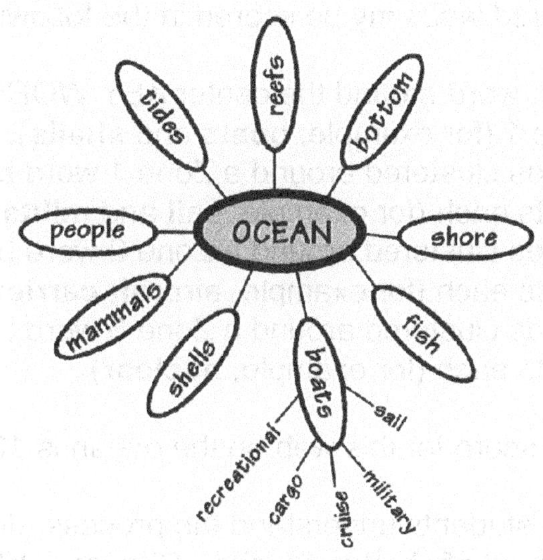

Think of these additions as KEY WORDS and continue the brainstorming from these words or any other words. From **cargo**, add the words **oil tankers** and **container ships.** From **military** add **aircraft carrier, mine sweeper** and **submarine**. From **submarine**, add **nuclear**.

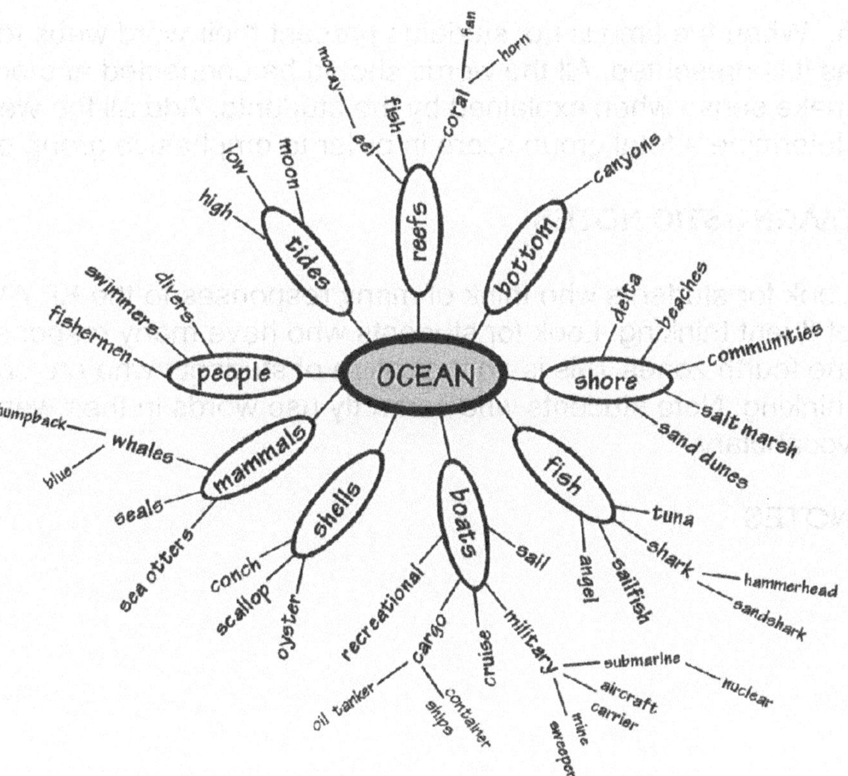

Add words to any cluster or part of the web at any time during the brainstorming. Allow ten minutes for the group brainstorming process. After the time is up, no additional words may be added to the web.

3. If desired,webs my be scored in the following manner:

- Each word around the center KEY WORD scores 1 point. This is called Zone 1 (for example, **boats** and **shells**).
- Words clustered around a Zone 1 word become Zone 2 and score 2 points each (for example, **sail** and **military**).
- Words clustered around a Zone 2 word become Zone 3 and score 3 points each (for example, **aircraft carrier** and **submarine**).
- Words clustered around a Zone 3 word become Zone 4 and score 4 points each (for example, **nuclear**).

The total score for this web on the ocean is 107.

4. When students understand the process, divide the class into triads. Give each group a large sheet of chart or butcher. Choose a KEY WORD. KEY WORDS should be a concept and something students know about. Possible KEY WORDS include forest, farm, space, or zoo. Students write the word at the center of their paper. Remind them that they will have 10 minutes to brainstorm.

5. When the time is up, students present their word webs to the class. Score each web as it is presented. All the words should be connected and only score those words which make sense when explained by the students. Add all the web scores together to determine a total group score in order to emphasize group effectiveness.

DIAGNOSTIC NOTES

Look for students who think of many responses to the KEY WORD. This is an indication of fluent thinking. Look for students who have many responses in the third and possibly the fourth zones.This is an indication of students who are capable of elaborative thinking. Note students who correctly use words in their web that indicate an advanced vocabulary.

NOTES

Web Magic

		Group #1 1. 2. 3.		Group #2 1. 2. 3.		Group #3 1. 2. 3.		Group #4 1. 2. 3.	
		# of words	score	# of words	score	# of words	score	# of words	score
Zone 1	x1								
Zone 2	x2								
Zone 3	x3								
Zone 4	x4								
Zone 5	x5								
Zone 6	x6								
Zone 7	x7								
Totals									

Grand Total

The Way to
Visual Thinking
1.
Look at things in different ways.
2.
Use what you see as clues.
3.
Move shapes around in your mind.
4.
Recognize patterns.
merritt 00

In this unit, students are presented with the concepts of visual thinking. This type of thinking, often neglected in traditional school work, is necessary in a variety of daily activities and is a vital part of many occupations. In this type of thinking, students use their right brain hemispheres to analyze shapes in unusual detail, manipulate shapes mentally, and recognize patterns.

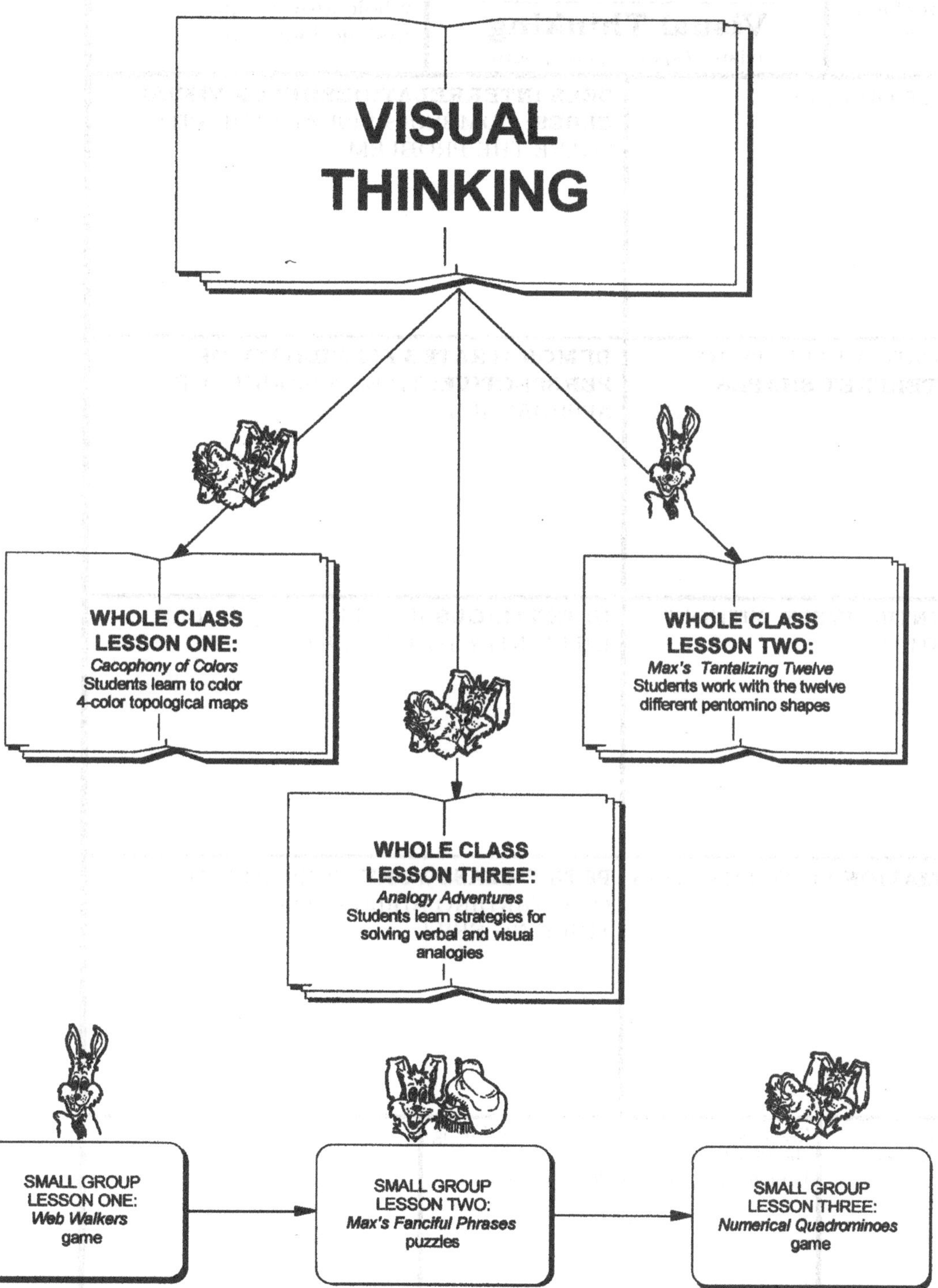

VISUAL THINKING

List names of students as each behavior appears.

Add checkmarks after name if behavior is repeated.

Use a different color of ink or pencil for each whole group lesson.

PETS™

Behavioral Checklist

Visual Thinking

(visual/spatial perception)

Teacher ________________
Grade _____

Dates of whole group instruction: 1. _______ 2. 3. _______

GRASPS CONCEPTS QUICKLY	**SEES INTERRELATIONSHIP OF VISUAL CLUES;** COMBINES VISUAL CLUES TO SOLVE THE PROBLEM
COMMENTS INDICATE AN ABILITY TO **MANIPULATE/INTERPRET SHAPES MENTALLY**	**DEMONSTRATES FLEXIBILITY OF PERSPECTIVE;** TRIES A VARIETY OF APPROACHES
SEES ANSWERS INTUITIVELY WITHOUT INTERMEDIATE STEPS	**IS TENACIOUS** IN APPROACH; WORKS DILIGENTLY TO THE END
RETAINS INFORMATION FROM PREVIOUS LESSONS	**PETS™ CLASSWORK** INDICATES AN OUTSTANDING ABILITY TO USE THIS THINKING SKILL

I see these behaviors in these students regularly during class time as well:	These students did not stand out during the PETS™ lessons, but I see these behaviors during regular class time:	Notes:

DIAGNOSTIC NOTES • VISUAL THINKING

<table>
<tr>
<td>GRASPS CONCEPTS QUICKLY
♦ sees perceptions presented quickly
♦ applies understanding to other situations quickly
♦ first to figure out correct answers</td>
<td>SEES INTERRELATIONSHIP OF VISUAL CLUES; COMBINES VISUAL CLUES TO SOLVE THE PROBLEM
♦ combines information from various visual clues to establish the pattern</td>
</tr>
<tr>
<td>COMMENTS INDICATE AN ABILITY TO MANIPULATE/INTERPRET SHAPES MENTALLY
♦ "sees" the shapes and/or the solution without needing to draw pictures or move puzzle pieces excessively</td>
<td>DEMONSTRATES FLEXIBILITY OF PERSPECTIVE; TRIES A VARIETY OF APPROACHES
♦ thinks flexibly about shapes
♦ tries many approaches</td>
</tr>
<tr>
<td>SEES ANSWERS INTUITIVELY WITHOUT INTERMEDIATE STEPS
♦ arrives at correct answer without seeming to use intermediate steps
♦ not an impulsive guesser</td>
<td>IS TENACIOUS IN APPROACH; WORKS DILIGENTLY TO THE END
♦ works diligently to conclusion
♦ will NOT give up</td>
</tr>
<tr>
<td>RETAINS INFORMATION FROM PREVIOUS LESSONS
♦ shares knowledge accurately during review
♦ applies knowledge during activities</td>
<td>PETS™ CLASSWORK INDICATES AN OUTSTANDING ABILITY TO USE THIS THINKING SKILL
♦ seatwork and/or challenge papers are exceptionally well done</td>
</tr>
</table>

I see these behaviors in these students regularly during class time as well:	These students did not stand out during the PETS™ lessons, but I see these behaviors during regular class time:	Notes:
♦ *normally great visual thinkers*	♦ *normally great visual thinkers who "hid out" during the PETS™ lesson*	♦ *absentees* ♦ *new students*

- *be generous — more inclusive than exclusive*
- *names can go in more than one box per answer*
- *be sure to add ✓s after names for multiple answers*
- *be sure to use different colors for each whole group lesson*

VISUAL THINKING
WHOLE CLASS
LESSON 1

PURPOSE

This lesson introduces students to the Four-Color Map Theorem with an opportunity to solve visual problems as they attempt to color maps using only four different colors.

MATERIALS

For projection:
- – *The Way to Visual Thinking* signpost
- – *Crystal Pond Woods Map 1*
- – *Crystal Pond Woods Map 2*

For duplication:
- – the story *Cacophony of Colors* to read aloud
- – class set of *Crystal Pond Woods Map 3*
- – class set of *From the Ground Up*
- – PETS™ *Behavioral Checklist - Visual Thinking*

– colored pencils or crayons for each student

LESSON PLAN

1. Review with students the guidelines for convergent and divergent thinking. If students have completed **PRIMARY EDUCATION THINKING SKILLS 1** and **PRIMARY EDUCATION THINKING SKILLS 2**, they have learned about visual thinking. Max the Magician uses his right brain hemisphere to visualize things mentally. He also uses convergent and divergent thinking when solving visual puzzles. The guidelines for visual thinking are listed below and are provided on *The Way to Visual Thinking* signpost. The term **visual thinking** as well as the following guidelines are presented in the story *Cacophony of Colors*:

- Look at things in different ways.
- Use what you see as clues.
- Move shapes around in your mind.
- Recognize patterns.

2. This lesson introduces students to the Four-Color Map Theorem, a mathematical application use in the field of topology. The theorem states that no more than four colors are ever needed to color the regions of any map so that no adjoining areas are the same color. Some simpler maps may be colored in fewer colors, but four colors will be

adequate to color any map. Although the need for four colors has been known to mathematicians since the 19th century, the theorem was not proven until 1976 and was the first mathematical theorem to be proven with the aid of computers.

3. Read the story *Cacophony of Colors* aloud. In the story, the characters color two easy maps of Crystal Pond Woods, which will be projected and modeled. The last two maps in the story are more difficult. A trouble spot on the Crystal Pond Woods Map 3 is mentioned in the story. The trouble spot is the region of the map labeled **forest** because this region wraps around three other regions requiring the regions to be four different colors.

4. If possible, students should use colored pencils. It is helpful if students use four distinctly different colors as opposed to four different shades of the same color. Remind students that it is NOT necessary, and may even hamper their work, to color the areas in appropriate colors. The pond does not have to be blue and the trees do not have to be green. Extra copies of the maps may be needed in case students need to start over. Note students who plan ahead using dots of color to determine if the colors are going to work.

5. Several extensions to the Four-Color Map Theorem can be given to students who are interested in the extra challenge. One extension is to color the outside border of the map one of the four colors. This is challenging because any shape on the border must be a different color than the outside. Another challenge is to ask students to draw a map which cannot be colored in four colors but must be done in five colors. This cannot be done and must be discovered by students on their own.

CHALLENGE PAGE

From the Ground Up

6. *From the Ground Up* is the challenge page for this lesson. This visual is also a "map." Ask students to consider what it might be. It is a close-up of a leaf in Crystal Pond Woods!

DIAGNOSTIC NOTES

The following is a short summary of what to look for in student behaviors and responses for Visual Thinking, Whole Class Lesson 1:

GRASPS CONCEPTS QUICKLY - Look for students who quickly color their maps and do not seem to need to plan, yet still color the map correctly.

SEES INTERRELATIONSHIP OF VISUAL CLUES - Look for students who will use all available clues. Unlike the student who intuitively approaches the problem, this student

may appear as a planner, analyzing the whole picture and making notations first before coloring.

VISUALIZES/MANIPULATES SHAPES MENTALLY - Note any students who create a correct solution without making many corrections. They may be seeing a finished map in their minds as they color.

DEMONSTRATES FLEXIBILITY OF PERSPECTIVE - Look for students who think flexibly about the maps and try many approaches. They may discover that working left to right across the map is not the best way to approach the problem and try a new approach.

SEES ANSWERS INTUITIVELY - Look for students who just seem to know how to color the maps correctly. These students may not be able to explain how they just "knew" it.

IS TENACIOUS - Students who "don't get it" have a tendency to give up easily. Look for students who have a tolerance for ambiguity and who persevere to reach a solution. Note students who derive a great amount of excitement from these activities as that often reflects an ability to solve such visual-spatial problems..

RETAINS INFORMATION - When reviewing ideas from earlier lessons, look for students who clearly recall the concepts and then effectively apply them to the current lesson's activities. While many children may grasp concepts "in the moment" of the instructional lesson, these students exhibit the significant ability to retain and apply new learning across time.

From The Ground Up

Note students who color the page correctly using only four colors. When possible, note those students who developed strategies to complete the activity. Note students who determined a creative response to the question *What is this?!*

NOTES

Cacophony of Colors

Sybil the Scientist was walking home one day when she noticed Max the Magician furiously drawing and coloring on his notepad. There were several discarded sheets of paper on the ground all around him. Being ever so curious, Sybil walked over to where Max sat and asked, "Max, whatever are you doing? I hope it's another one of your challenging puzzles!"

"Oh, hi, Sybil," replied Max as he looked up at her. "Yes, I'm working on a very perplexing puzzle and maybe you can help me."

"You know I love puzzles, too, and I'd be glad to help," answered Sybil as she sat down next to Max. "You're such a good **visual thinker**, Max! Will you review with me the guidelines for visual thinking?" continued Sybil as she pointed to **The Way to Visual Thinking** signpost.

*(Project **The Way to Visual Thinking** signpost.)*

"Visual thinkers try to see things in their heads, to view things mentally," began Max. "Visual thinkers **look at things in different ways**. You have to **use what you see as clues**. Sometimes a visual thinker has to **move the shapes around in his or her head**, trying to see what it looks like. And finally, visual thinkers are always looking for **patterns**."

"I'm good at recognizing patterns! That's one of the things that scientists do!" exclaimed Sybil. "Show me your puzzle!"

"It started out very easy," explained Max. "I wanted to make a map of Crystal Pond Woods and color it in such a way that regions next to each other are different colors. The challenge is that I only have four colored pencils. I started out with this simple map which included the woods and the pond."

*(Project **Crystal Pond Woods Map 1**.)*

"That's an easy map to color," said Sybil as she picked up two colored pencils and colored each region a different color.

(Color the map using two different colors.)

"Yes, it is easy," agreed Max. "However, since I want my map to be more detailed, I added the meadow and Isabel's oak tree."

*(Project **Crystal Pond Woods Map 2**.)*

"As you can see, Sybil, it's going to take three colors to color this map so that the woods, meadow and pond, which all border each other, are a different color," pointed out Max.

"What about the oak tree?" wondered Sybil.

"I can color that the same as the meadow or the pond since they don't touch," replied Max as he began coloring.

*(Color **Crystal Pond Woods Map 2** using three different colors.)*

"Now," Max continued, "look at this map that I've drawn which is an even more detailed map."

*(Project **Crystal Pond Woods Map 3**.)*

"I tried coloring this map with only three different colors, and it might have worked except for one trouble spot."

Sybil stared at the map for a bit, then looked at the **Visual Thinking** signpost. "If I **use what I see as clues**, I think I see the trouble spot. This forest area is going to require at least four colors because of the way this area wraps around the others. *(Point to the word **forest**.)* Three colors will not be enough."

"Yes," agreed Max. "That is the exact spot where I had trouble coloring the map and had to use a fourth color. I was starting to color this map when you walked over. Will you help me finish the map so I know whether or not four colors are going to be enough?"

"Of course, Max! I wouldn't be able to leave until I know whether or not this puzzle of the colors can be solved."

*(Give students a copy of **Crystal Pond Woods Map 3** to color using only four colors. Suggest that students use colored pencils and place a dot in each region before actually coloring. It will be much easier for students to*

make any necessary changes. The remainder of the story provides some background on the Four-Color Map Theorem and can be read while students are working.)

"That was fun, Max!" said Sybil as they finished coloring the map.

"What if we added even more details to the map, Sybil?" wondered Max. "Do you think we would need to use five colors to color it?"

Intrigued by this question, Max and Sybil began to add details to the map. Jordan happened to notice the two busy at work and joined them, asking what they were working on.

"We've drawn a detailed map of Crystal Pond Woods and are trying to see if we can color the map so that regions next to each other are different colors. We don't know if we're going to need four colors or if it's going to take more than four colors," explained Max.

Jordan pondered this a minute. "I recently read an article in a mathematics journal about just this type of problem. Any map can be colored just the way you describe, and you will never need more than four colors. It's a very famous mathematical puzzle."

"Wow, that's cool!" Max exclaimed. "And it means that I don't need to go and get another colored pencil to color this map. My four colors will be enough!"

"Even though you have the correct number of colors, Max," Sybil pointed out, "I don't think it means that this is now an easy problem to solve. I've been studying this map and I think that using your four colors is going to be very challenging!"

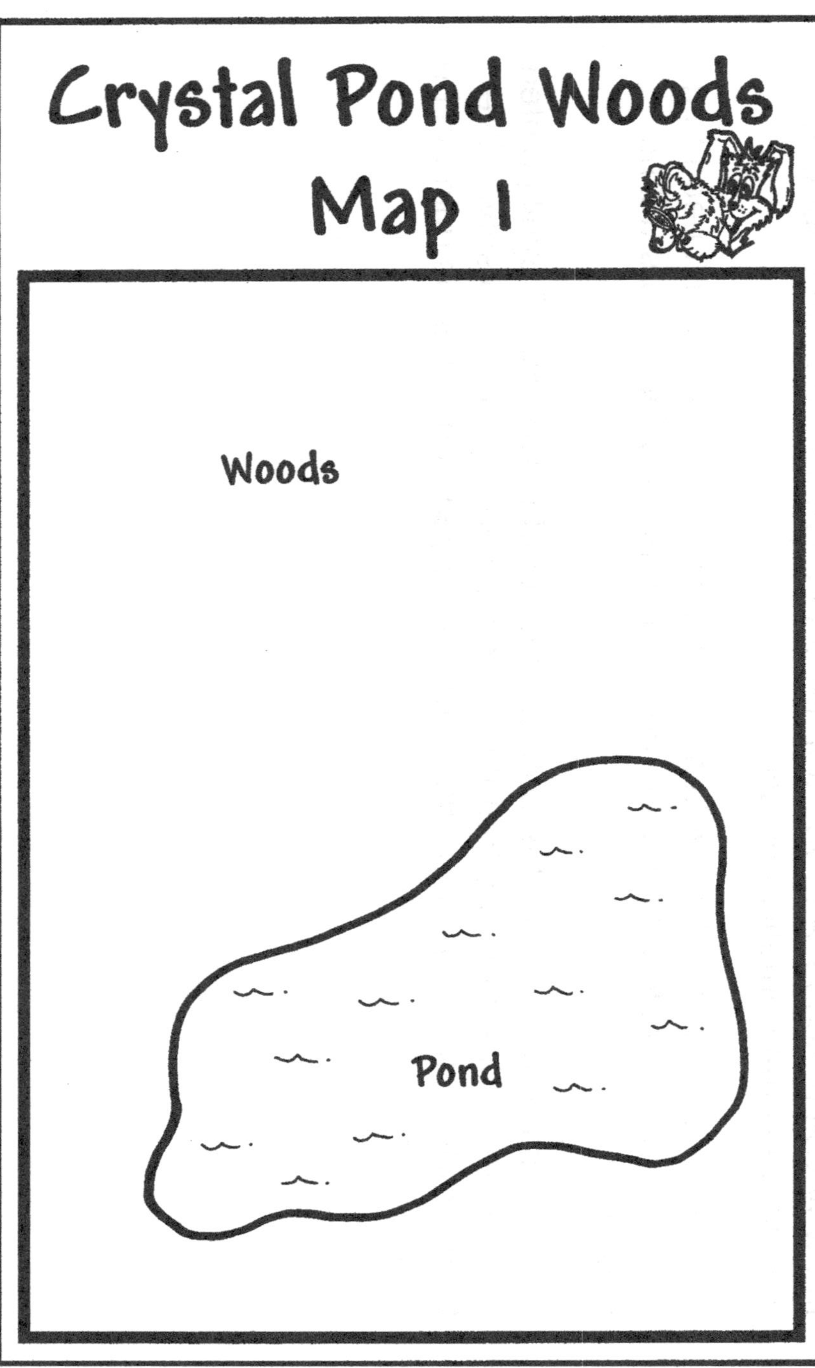

Crystal Pond Woods Map 1

Woods
Pond

Crystal Pond Woods Map 2

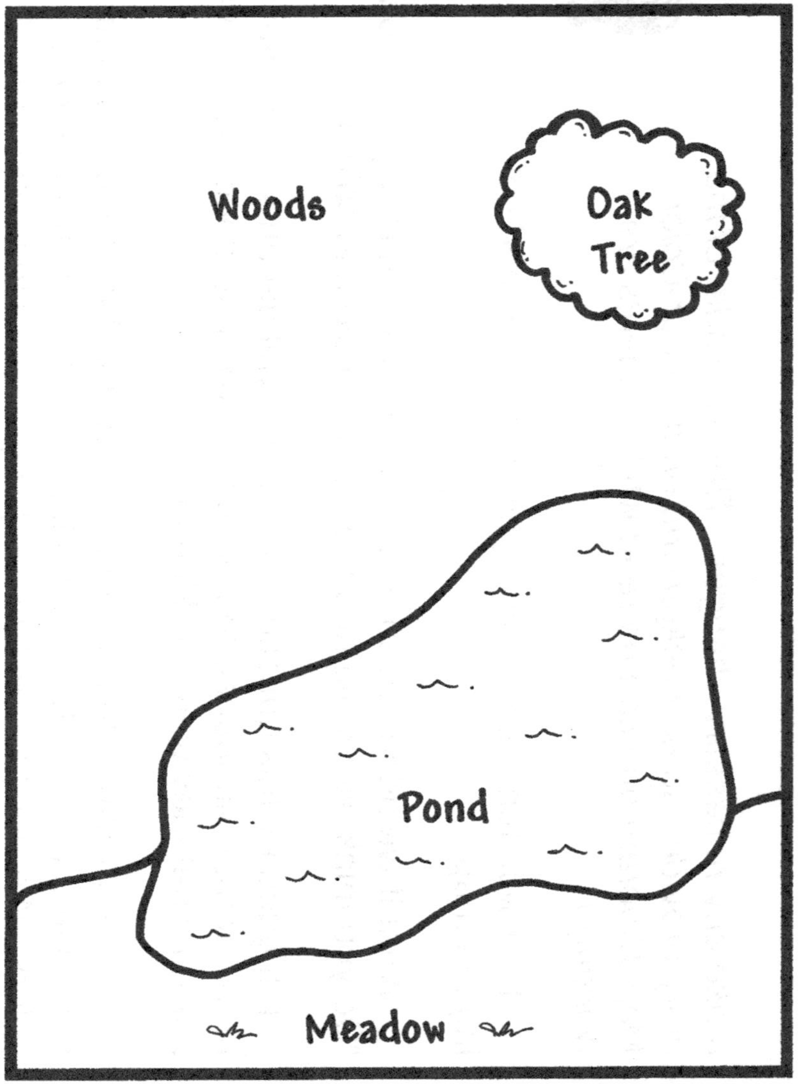

Woods
Oak Tree
Pond
Meadow

Name ______________________________

Crystal Pond Woods: Map 3

Here is the third map of Crystal Pond Woods drawn by Max and Sybil. Color in all the areas. You may use only 4 different colors. Make sure that no two areas that share a side are the same color.

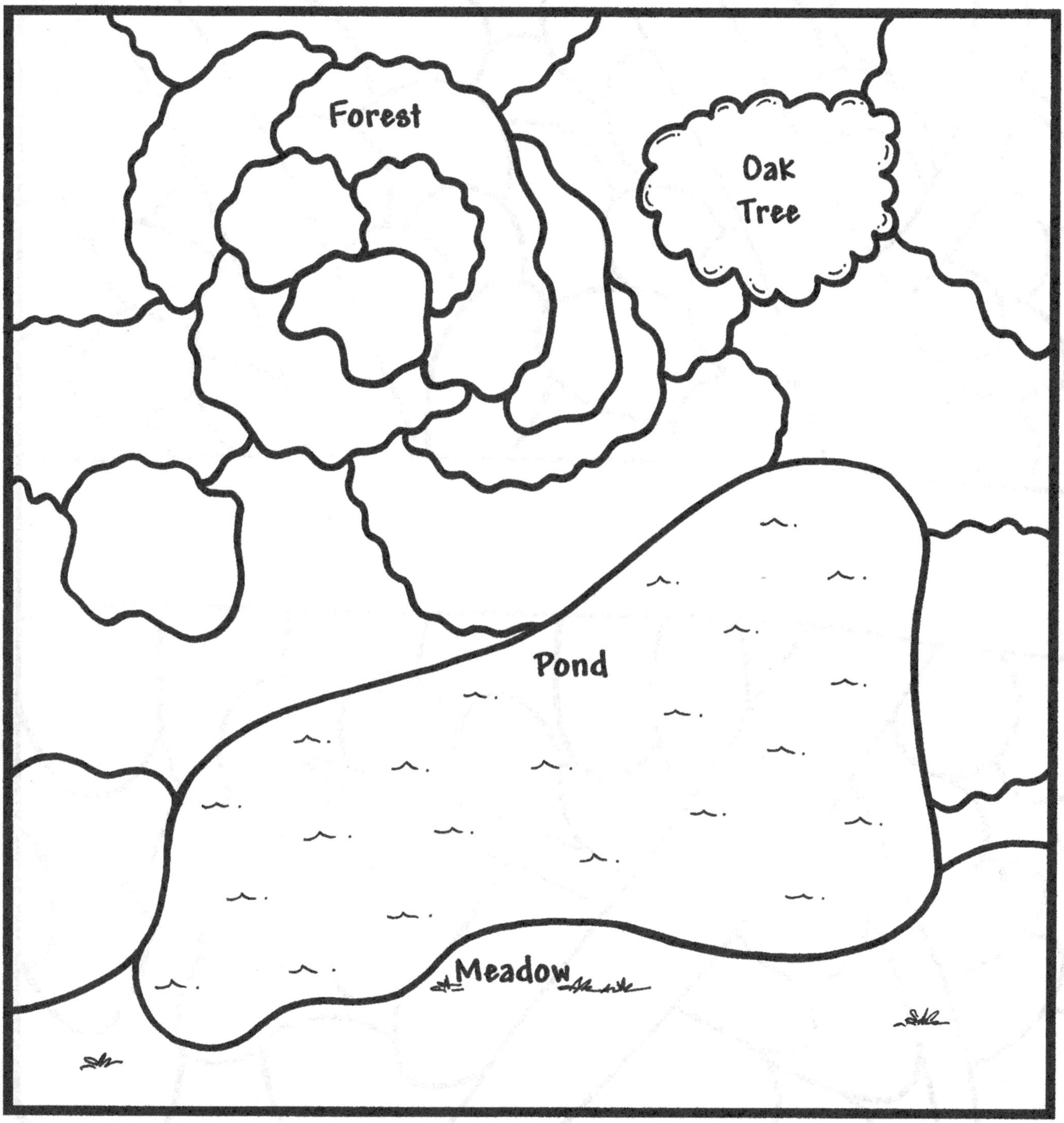

Name ______________________________

From the Ground Up

Color in all the areas. You may use only 4 different colors. Make sure that no two areas that share a side are the same color.

What *is* this?!

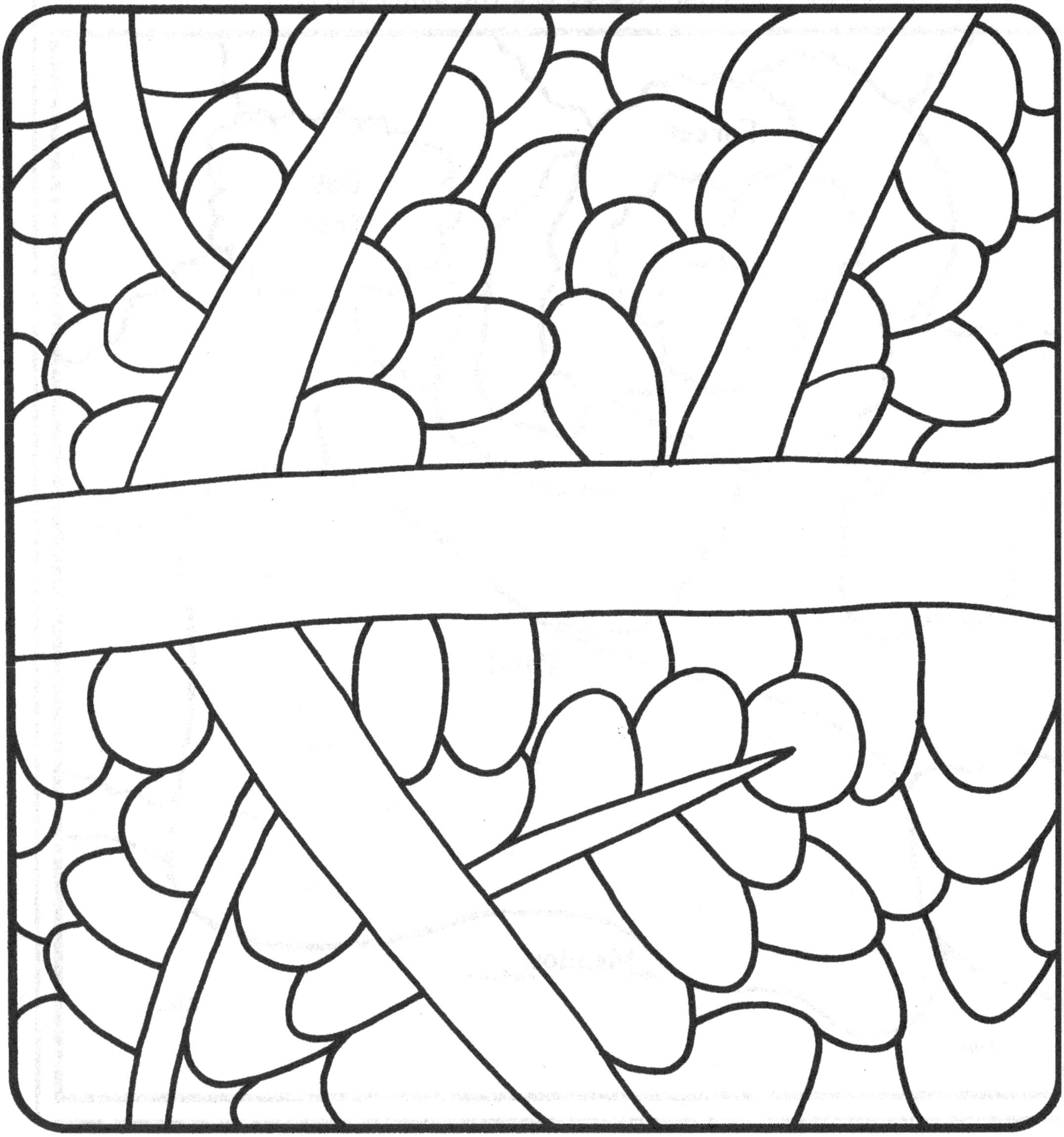

VISUAL THINKING
WHOLE CLASS
LESSON 2

PURPOSE

The purpose of this lesson is to develop the concepts of visual thinking through the manipulation of shapes. Students will manipulate pentomino shapes to solve a variety of puzzles.

MATERIALS

For projection:
- *The Way to Visual Thinking* signpost

For duplication:
- the story *Max's Tantalizing Twelve* to read aloud
- class set of *Do It Twice!*
- class set of *Animal Friends*
- class set of *Crystal Pond...*
- class set of *...Woods*
- *PETS™ Behavioral Checklist - Visual Thinking*

– a set of pentominoes for each student (either a commercial set OR a set made from *Max's Snapshot* and *Dudley's Snapshot)*

LESSON PLAN

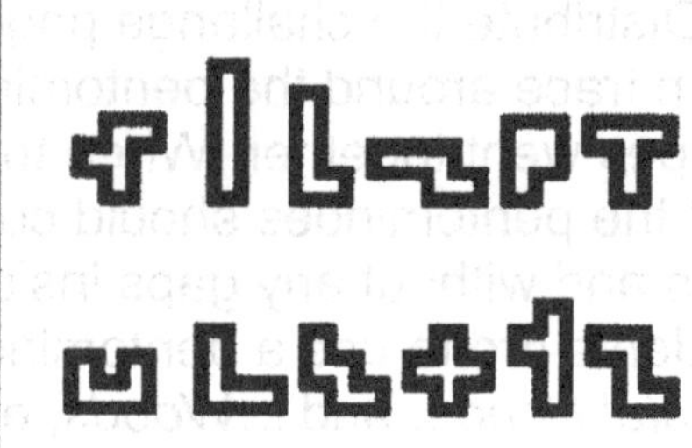

1. Visual Thinking, Whole Class Lesson 2 involves manipulating the twelve pentomino shapes. Discovering the twelve pentomino shapes is a fun and challenging activity to do as an introductory lesson. Pentominoes are shapes formed from five unit squares. Edges of the squares must align evenly so that corners match up. *Max's Snapshot* and *Dudley's Snapshot* provide an answer key for all twelve of the pentomino shapes. In order to discover the twelve pentominoes, students need square graph paper on which to draw the outlines of the pentominoes. The simplest pentomino is the 1 x 5 rectangle. As students try to find the twelve pentominoes, be aware that flips and rotations are not new shapes. If students claim to find more than twelve pentominoes, there are probably duplicate shapes that have been flipped or rotated. This activity may take 30 to 45 minutes, and if done, should be a separate lesson.

2. Review with students the guidelines for visual thinking using *The Way to Visual Thinking* signpost:

- Look at things in different ways.
- Use what you see as clues.
- Move shapes around in your mind.
- Recognize patterns.

3. Students will be manipulating the pentomino pieces. The activities have been designed so that commercial pentomino sets may be used. If commercial sets are not available, make the pentomino sets prior to the lesson. Pentomino die cuts may also be used to make a pentomino set for each student. Die cutting on cover stock or craft foam provides very durable sets. To make the pentominoes using the lesson materials, copy *Max's Snapshot* and *Dudley's Snapshot* on cover stock. Have students carefully cut out the pieces and place them in an envelope. The puzzle sets can be laminated for use year after year.

4. Read the story *Max's Tantalizing Twelve* aloud to students. The story reviews some of the visual thinking guidelines and introduces the pentominoes to students. It is shorter than most of the stories so that students have more time to work on the puzzles.

5. Give students a set of pentominoes. If students are using the pentominoes from *Max's Snapshot* and *Dudley's Snapshot*, one activity is to put the pieces back together to form Max and Dudley. If this is the first experience students have had with pentominoes, they will need a few minutes to explore and examine the pieces.

CHALLENGE PAGES

Do It Twice! *Animal Friends* *Crystal Pond...* *. . . Woods*

6. Distribute the challenge pages. Once students have correctly covered a puzzle, have them trace around the pentominoes on the paper so they have a record of how the shapes went together. When the directions ask students to fill the shapes, this means that the pentominoes should cover the entire shape without going over the boundary lines and without any gaps inside. When completing *Do It Twice!* and *Animal Friends*, students are to use a pentomino piece only once on each page. When completing *Crystal Pond...* and *...Woods*, each letter is a different puzzle and students may "start over" pentomino use with each letter. Please note that the vertical line inside the **P** shape should be ignored when covering the shape with pentominoes. An extension to the lesson is to have students make the largest rectangle or square possible using one set of pentominoes.

ANSWER KEY

Do It Twice!

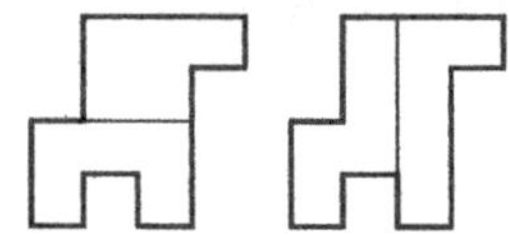

Animal Friends

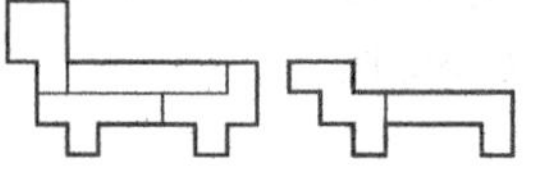

Crystal Ponds Woods

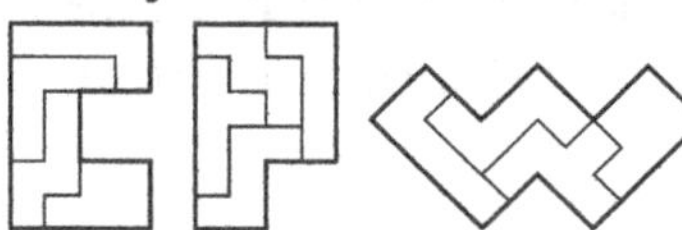

DIAGNOSTIC NOTES

The following is a short summary of what to look for in student behaviors and responses for Visual Thinking, Whole Class Lesson 2:

GRASPS CONCEPTS QUICKLY - Look for students who quickly solve the puzzles. Note everytime a student correctly completes a puzzle.

SEES INTERRELATIONSHIP OF VISUAL CLUES - Look for students who will use all available clues. The comments made as students work are excellent indicators of their thinking processes. Record students whose comments depict good spatial reasoning.

VISUALIZES/MANIPULATES SHAPES MENTALLY - Note any students who solve a puzzle very quickly without excessive manipulation of the pentomino pieces. Possible indicators of mental manipulation of shapes would be students who tilt or turn their heads as they work.

DEMONSTRATES FLEXIBILITY OF PERSPECTIVE - Look for students who think flexibly about the puzzles and are willing to try many approaches to solving the puzzles.

SEES ANSWER INTUITIVELY - Look for students who just seem to know how the pentomino pieces go together. Those students may work very quickly yet accurately.

IS TENACIOUS - Students who “don’t get it” have a tendency to give up easily. Look for students who have a tolerance for ambiguity and who persevere to reach a solution. Note students who derive a great amount of excitement from these activities as that often reflects an ability to solve such visual-spatial problems.

RETAINS INFORMATION – When reviewing ideas from earlier lessons, look for students who clearly recall the concepts and then effectively apply them to the current lesson's activities. While many children may grasp concepts "in the moment" of the instructional lesson, these students exhibit the significant ability to retain and apply new learning across time.

Max's Tantalizing Twelve

Max the Magician had a project this morning. Last night he had played dominoes with his Crystal Pond Woods companions. Because he **looks at things in different ways**, Max wanted to create a new puzzle based on the idea of dominoes. Dominoes are made by putting two squares together. Max decided to put five squares together in as many ways as possible.

"Good morning, Max!" greeted Yolanda the Yarnspinner as she dropped in from the tree above. "I can see that you are thinking hard this morning. Are you working on a puzzle for us to solve at the campfire tonight?"

"Of course," smiled Max. "I've been trying to **move these shapes around in my head**. I'm using five squares to make shapes for a puzzle. I think there are twelve ways to put the shapes together but I want to check out some **patterns** to make sure I didn't miss any shapes."

"These are very unique shapes," noted Yolanda as she studied the shapes. "What are you going to call them?"

"I don't know," said Max looking up in surprise. "I haven't thought of that yet."

"I have a suggestion," Yolanda said thoughtfully. "These shapes remind me of the dominoes we played with last night and they are made with five squares. A pentagon has five sides and since these are made five squares, why not call them pentominoes?!"

"Pentominoes ... what a great name! You are so good with words, Yolanda!" exclaimed Max. "Now that I have the twelve pentomino shapes figured out, would you like to stay and help me design the puzzles?"

"No, thank you. I would much rather DO your puzzles tonight at the campfire!" replied Yolanda as she smiled and spun away.

Max's Snapshot

Max
the
Magician

(This Snapshot supplies 6 of Max's 12 pentominoes)

Dudley's Snapshot

Dudley the Detective

DETECTIVE DUDLEY

(This Snapshot supplies 6 of Max's 12 pentominoes)

Name ______________________________

Do It Twice!

Fill both these shapes with some up Max's pentominoes. Do not use any piece more than once on this page. Trace your solutions.

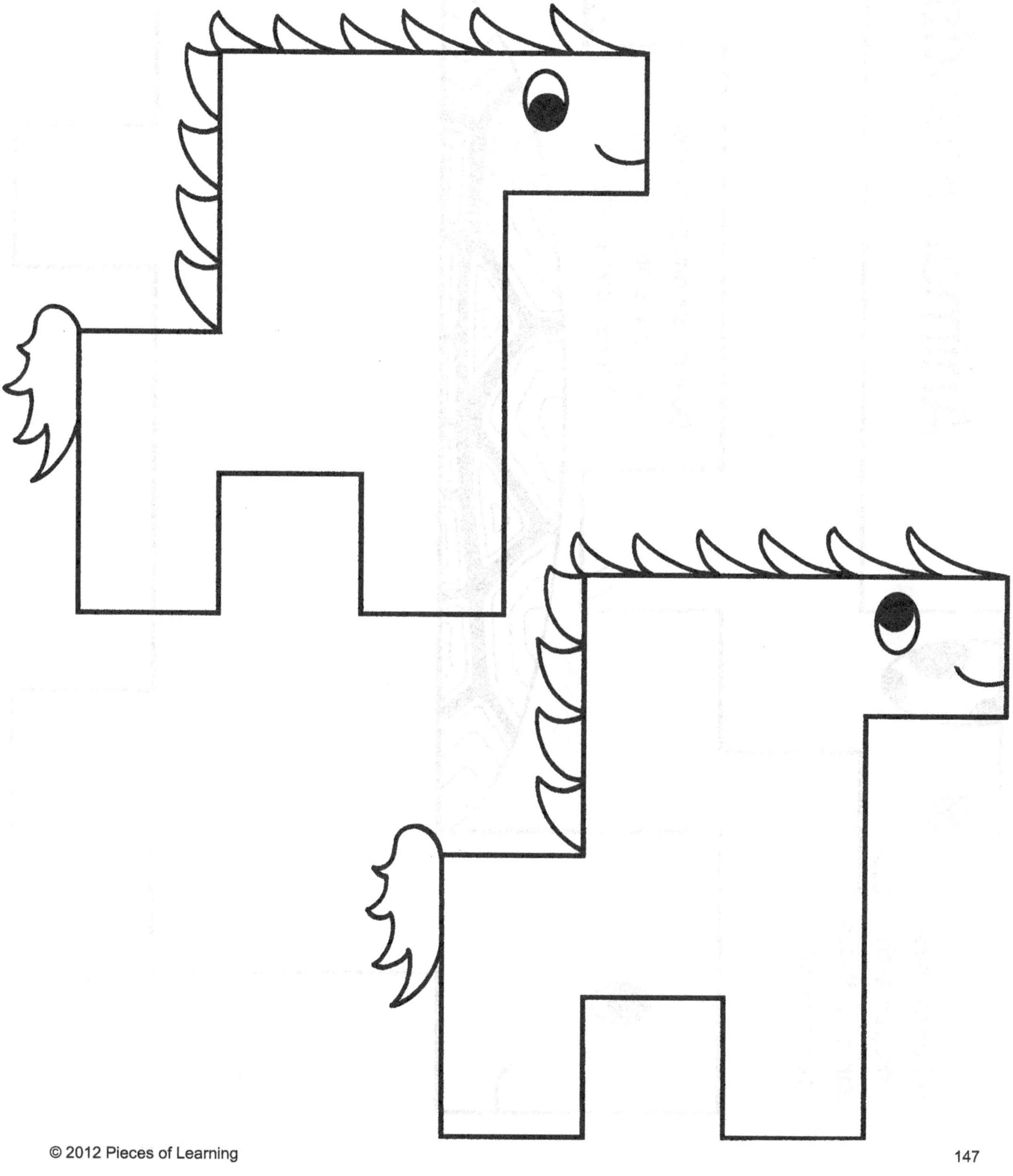

Animal Friends

Name ______________________________

Fill both these shapes with some of Max's pentominoes.

Do not use any piece more than once on this page. Trace your solutions.

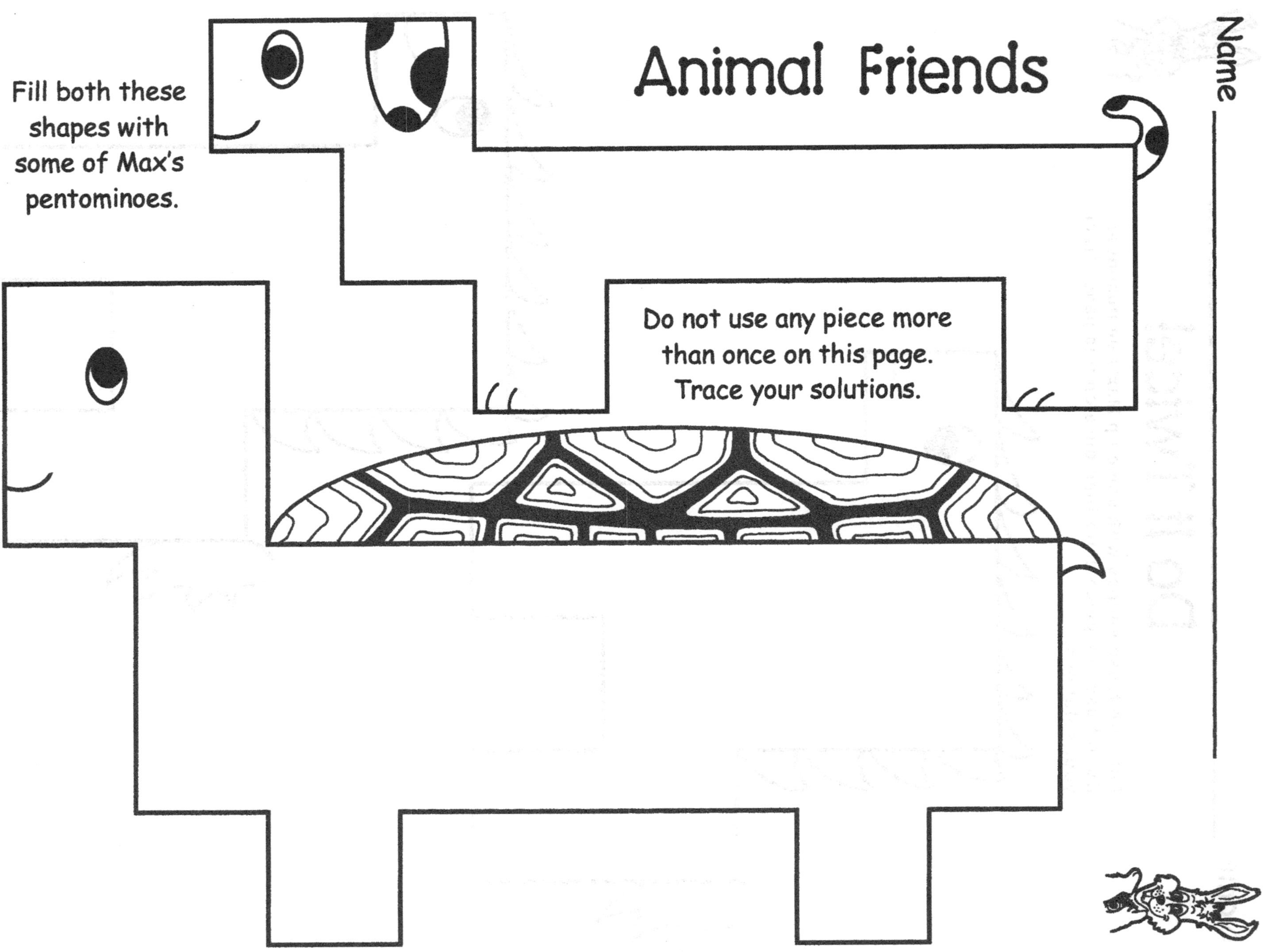

Name ______________________________

Crystal Pond ...

Fit Max's pentominoes into these letters.

Name ______________________________

Use any of Max's twelve pentomino pieces to fill this letter.

...Woods

VISUAL THINKING
WHOLE CLASS
LESSON 3

PURPOSE

The purpose of this lesson is to give students an opportunity to analyze visual analogies.

MATERIALS

For projection:

– *The Way to Visual Thinking* signpost
– *Analogy Analysis*

For duplication:

– the story *Analogy Adventures* to read aloud
– class set of *Analogy Adventures 1*
– class set of *Analogy Adventures 2*
– class set of *Analogy Adventures 3*
– class set of *Analogy Adventures 4*
– *PETS™ Behavioral Checklist - Visual Thinking*

LESSON PLAN

1. Review with students the guidelines of visual thinking using *The Way to Visual Thinking* signpost:

- Look at things in different ways.
- Use what you see as clues.
- Move shapes around in your mind.
- Recognize patterns.

2. Read the story *Analogy Adventures* aloud. In the story, Yolanda teaches Max how to interpret and write word analogies. Three visual analogies are part of the story. If students are able to figure out the correct solution and explain why that is the answer, it is not necessary to read the entire story. Instruction on the various types of visual analogies is provided in the story and will be needed for the challenge pages. If students are able to determine the correct answer but are not able to explain their reasoning, it is important to read the story explanation.

CHALLENGE PAGES

Analogy Adventures 1 *Analogy Adventures 2*
Analogy Adventures 3 *Analogy Adventures 4*

3. Distribute challenge pages to students. These analogies use rotations, slides, and eliminations as well as combinations of these strategies.

ANSWER KEY *Analogy Adventures*:

1:		*2*:		*3*:		*4*:	
	1. B		1. C		1. B		1. A
	2. D		2. B		2. D		2. C
	3. A		3. D		3. C		3. A
	4. D		4. B		4. A		4. B
	5. A		5. A		5. D		5. C

DIAGNOSTIC NOTES

The following is a short summary of what to look for in student behaviors and responses for Visual Thinking, Whole Class Lesson 3:

GRASPS CONCEPTS QUICKLY - Look for students who quickly see how to accurately solve visual analogies.

SEES INTERRELATIONSHIP OF VISUAL CLUES - Look for students who will use all available clues. They may be seen going back and forth from one shape to another in the analogy.

VISUALIZES/MANIPULATES SHAPES MENTALLY - Students who are adept at mentally manipulating shapes may tilt their head from side to side or draw in the air with their pencils. Note students who seem to be visualizing mentally.

DEMONSTRATES FLEXIBILITY OF PERSPECTIVE - Look for students who think flexibly about the shapes and try many approaches.

SEE ANSWERS INTUITIVELY - Look for students who consistly seem to know the correct reponses to the analogies without being able to explain their reasoning.

IS TENACIOUS - Students who “don’t get it” have a tendency to give up easily. Look for students who have a tolerance for ambiguity and who persevere to reach a solution. Note students who derive a great amount of excitement from these activities as that often reflects an ability to solve such visual-spatial problems.

RETAINS INFORMATION – When reviewing ideas from earlier lessons, look for students who clearly recall the concepts and then effectively apply them to the current lesson's activities. While many children may grasp concepts "in the moment" of the instructional lesson, these students exhibit the significant ability to retain and apply new learning across time.

Analogy Adventures

One sunny afternoon, Max the Magician came hopping down a leaf-strewn path in Crystal Pond Woods to find his friend, Yolanda the Yarnspinner, hanging from **The Way to Visual Thinking** signpost with all eight legs busy at work furiously writing words on four pads of paper. "What are you doing?" Max inquired of his arachnid friend.

"Oh, hello, Max!" Yolanda replied. "You've caught me diverting myself with one of my favorite pastimes. I'm generating analogies. Next to creating exquisite, glistening webs, it's one of my best-loved amusements."

"Yolanda," Max sighed, "I always love to hear you talk. Your creative way of putting things fascinates me. What are analogies?"

"Analogies," explained Yolanda, "are comparisons between two similar pairs of items, in this case, of course, words. For example, '**Hat** is to **head** as **shoe** is to **foot**.' That's an analogy because the relationship between your hat and your head is the same as the relationship between your shoe and your foot."

"Oh, I see!" Max agreed. "I wear a shoe on my foot, the same as I wear a hat on my head! This is fun! Share some more with me!"

"I'll tell you what," suggested Yolanda. "I'll start you off, and you see if you can supply the last word in the relationship."

Max was even more excited at his friend's suggestion. "Like a game! I love the idea! Let's go!"

"OK....We'll start off easy, but some of these get tricky. You'll really have to wear your thinking hat."

Max adjusted his tall hat over his long ears. "I'm ready," he said.

Yolanda began. "**Net** is to **butterfly** as **pole** is to *blank.* You have to tell me what goes in the blank."

"I know!" cried Max. "Fish! You use a net to catch a butterfly, and you use a pole to catch a fish! Try another one."

"OK. **Wind** is to **kite** as **oar** is to *blank.* What goes in the blank?"

"Rowboat!" shouted Max. "Let's do a harder one."

"All right," Yolanda smiled, "if you think you're ready. **Ball** is to **circle** as **cone** is to *blank*."

"Triangle," said Max. "A ball is a three-dimensional circle, and a cone is a three-dimensional triangle. That was easy for me because I can visualize shapes so well. Yolanda, I like the idea of this game and you know that I like shapes and pictures as much as you like words. Can we do these with shapes?"

Yolanda agreed readily. "I don't see why not," she said. "We would just have to draw them as pictures instead of reading them out loud. Let me show you a shorthand way of doing it.

*(Project **Analogy Analysis** to demonstrate while reading the story. Cover all but example 1.)*

"Draw the first shape, for example, a tree. Then put two vertical dots, like a colon, after it. This is the symbol for 'is to.' Then draw your second shape, for example, a bird. Now this says 'Tree is to bird.' Next put two colons together in a square array. This is the symbol for 'as.' Draw your third shape now, for example, a lake. Then put another colon. Now, without words, this reads 'Tree is to bird as lake is to.' Then the other player just has to put the final picture in. I'd choose a fish."

"Great!" cried Max. "You really have to **use what you see as a clue**. Now it's my turn to challenge you! I'm going to **look at this in a different way** than you did!"

Max displayed his first set of three designs.

(Uncover example 2.)

"Can you guess which one goes in the last spot, Yolanda?" he asked.

(Solicit student responses. As students give answers, it is important that they explain why they chose the answer given. The following paragraph provides the answer, ***c****, and an explanation. If this has already been discussed, skip to example 3.)*

"I do see what you've constructed, Max," Yolanda replied instantly. "You rotated the first rectangular shape counter-clockwise 90 degrees, so I opt for **c**, the triangle which does the same rotation. I can determine it by taking note of the darkened portion. I had to **mentally move the shape** in my mind."

(Uncover example 3. Solicit student responses. The correct answer is ***b*** *and an explanation is given below.)*

Yolanda smiled instantly. "This one is elementary, too. See how the dark circle slides slightly to the right until it overlaps the square? That means the accurate response would be the one in which the dark triangle slides to the right to overlap the pentagon. Am I correct?"

"You are," Max agreed. "Here's a more complex design. I'll stump you this time!" He placed another set of designs under her eight eyes.

(Uncover example 4. Solicit student responses. The correct answer is ***d****.)*

"Hmmmm ... this design is more complex ... oh, look! In the second design, there is simply an arc eliminated from the bottom of the circle to change it from the first. I'll designate the answer that is the square with the bottom portion removed."

"You're right!" cried Max. "You're good at this game! Let's create some more so we can stump everyone at the campfire tonight."

Analogy Analysis

1\. : :: :

2\. : :: : ______

a. b. c. d.

3\. : :: : ______

a. b. c. d.

4\. : :: : ______

Name ______________________________

Analogy Adventures 1

1. 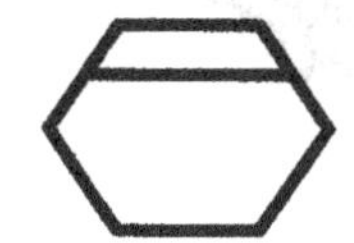 : 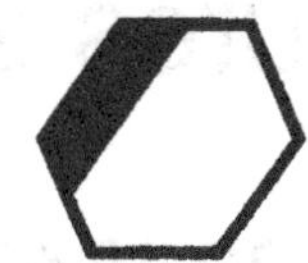 :: 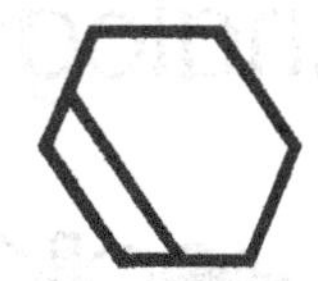 : ______

a. 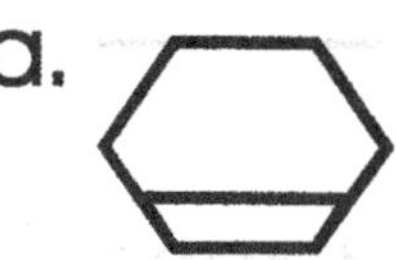 b. 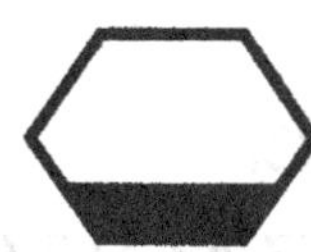 c.  d. 

2.  :  ::  : ______

a.  b.  c.  d. 

3.  :  :: 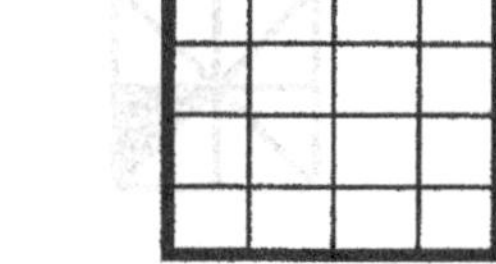 : ______

a.  b.  c. 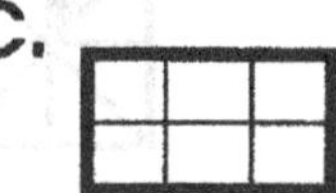 d. 

4.  :  ::  : ______

a.  b.  c.  d. 

5.  : ::  : ______

a.  b.  c. d. 

Name ______________________________

Analogy Adventures 2

1\. ◇▯▥●⬡○◀ : ◀●○▥◇⬡▯ :: 1234567 : ______

a. 2561437 b. 7654321 c. 7463152 d. 7564231

2\. 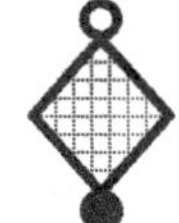 :  :: 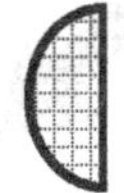 : ______

a.  b.  c. 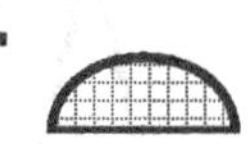 d. 

3\.  : 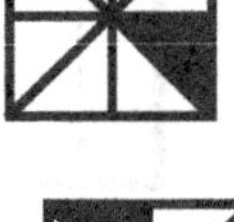 ::  : ______

a. b. c. d. 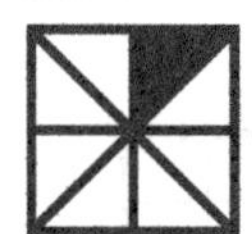

4\.  :  ::  : ______

a.  b.  c.  d.

5\. 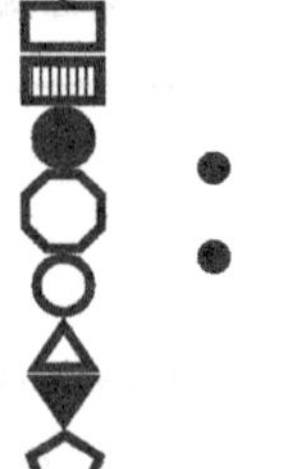

A B C D E F G H I

:  :: 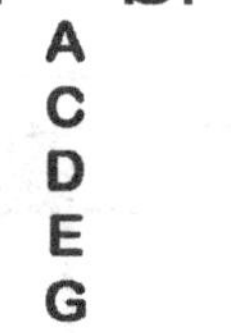 : ______

a.	b.	c.	d.
A	A	A	B
C	B	D	C
D	C	F	D
E	D	G	F
G	E	C	G
H	F	H	H
I	G	I	I

Name ______________________________

Analogy Adventures 3

1.  :  ::  : ______

a. b. c. d.

2.  :  ::  : ______

a.  b.  c.  d. 

3.  :  :: 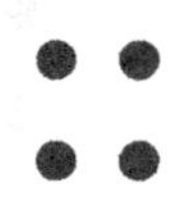  : ______

a. b. c. d. 

4. 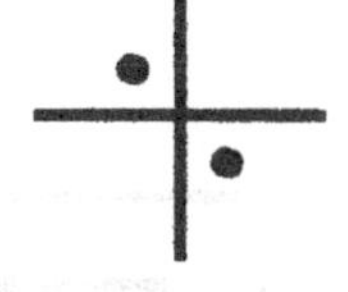 : ______

a.  b.  c.  d. 

5. **MONKEY** :  ::  **DONKEY** : ______

a.  b. c.  d.

Name ______________________________

Analogy Adventures 4

1.  :  :: 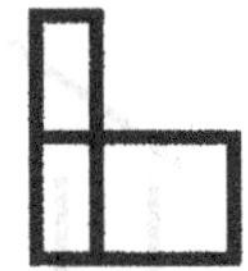 : ______

a. 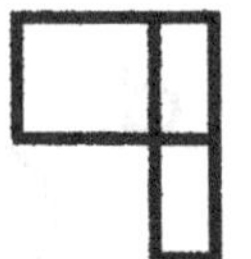 b.  c.  d. 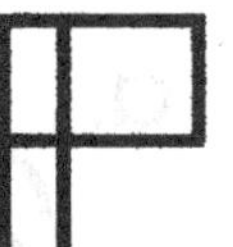

2.  :  ::  : ______

a.  b.  c.  d. 

3.  :  ::  : ______

a. b.  c.  d.  

4.   : :: : ______

a. b.  c.  d.  

5. pierce :  :: recipe : ______

a.  b.  c. d.

VISUAL THINKING SMALL GROUP LESSON 1

PURPOSE

The purpose of this lesson is to allow students an opportunity to use visual and convergent thinking as they develop effective strategies for the game *Web Walkers*.

MATERIALS

For duplication:

– *Web Walkers* game board for each pair of students
– *PETS™ Small Group Checklist* for each student

– a set of nine game pieces for each student

LESSON PLAN

1. *Web Walkers* is a strategy game for two players. The object of the game is to be the first player to reduce the opponent to only two game pieces or to block the opponent so that no further moves are possible. Each player needs nine game pieces. For example, one player may use nine blue chips and the other player nine red chips. The game begins with the first player placing a game piece on any of the circles on Yolanda's web. The other player then places a game piece on a circle on Yolanda's web. Taking turns, players continue placing game pieces on the board, one at a time, until all 18 game pieces are on Yolanda's web. When all of the game pieces have been placed on the board, players continue to alternate turns. A turn consists of moving one game piece along the web to an adjacent vacant circle. Players try to move their game pieces in an attempt to have three in a row along any of the straight lines of the web.

2. When a player has three game pieces in a straight row, he can immediately remove a game piece belonging to the opponent. This is also true during the placing of the game pieces at the beginning of the game. When a player has three in a row, any game piece belonging to the opponent may be taken unless it is part of an existing three in a row. A player may move a game piece out of his own three in a row and right back in on the next move, if he is not blocked from doing so.

3. Game pieces can only move along the web lines to adjacent vacant spaces until one of the players is down to only three game pieces. When this happens, the player with only three pieces may "fly" one of his game pieces to any vacant spot on the web. Flying allows a player who is close to losing a chance to redeem himself against an adversary with more game pieces. Flying is a last-ditch effort and the person with only

three game pieces may choose to fly or not on each subsequent turn. Flying forces the winning opponent to think a little harder and develop new strategies.

4. Winning is achieved when one's opponent is down to two game pieces, making it impossible to form three in a row, or when the opponent is boxed in so that she cannot make any moves at all.

DIAGNOSTIC NOTES

Look for students who seem to play the game in their heads, viewing future moves without having to manipulate the pieces. Also note students who consistently win. They may have developed strategies which they may or may not be able to verbalize. Listening to students while they are playing the game will provide additional diagnostic information.

NOTES

Web Walkers

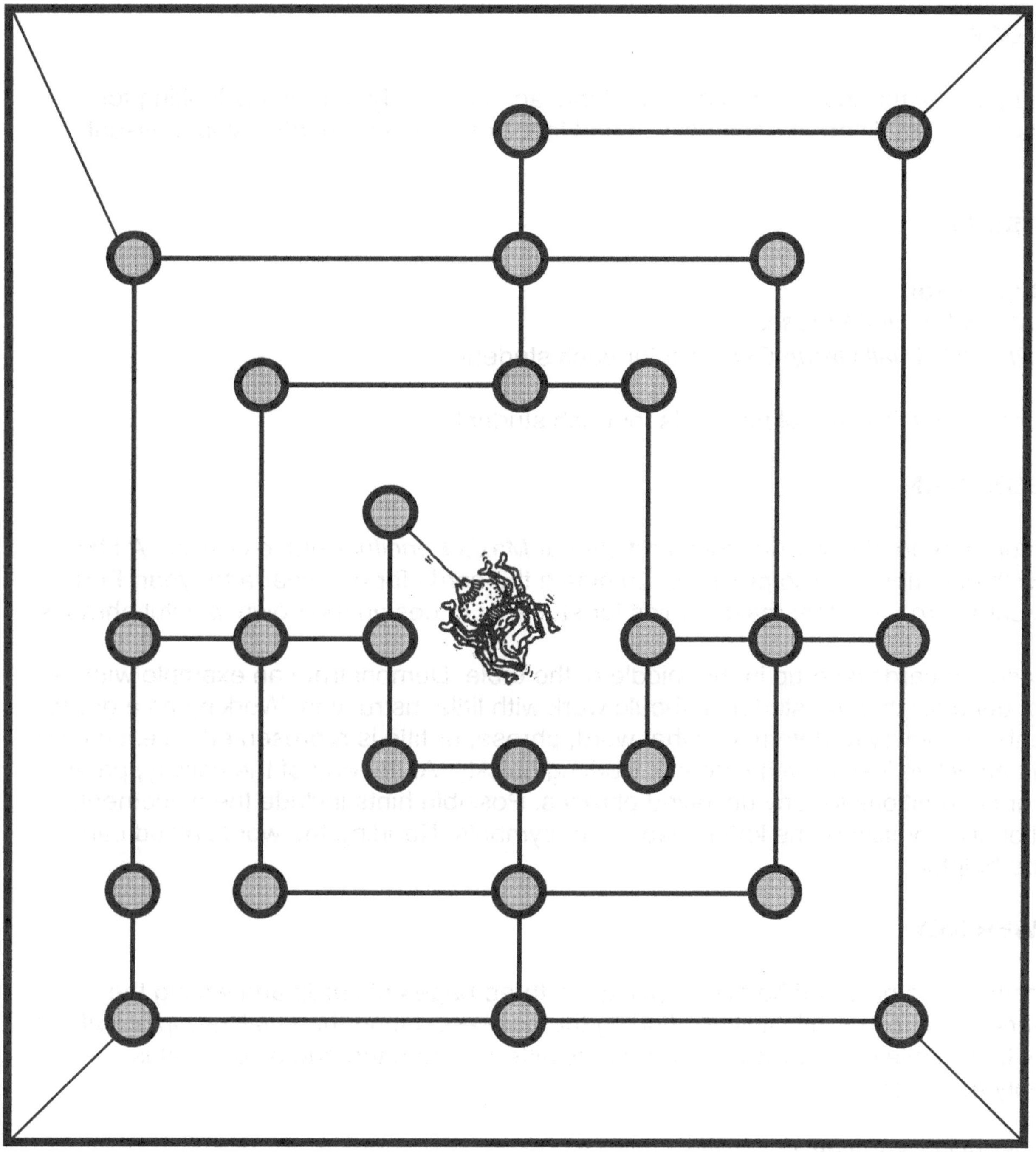

VISUAL THINKING SMALL GROUP LESSON 2

PURPOSE

The purpose of this lesson is to give students an opportunity to practice looking for visual clues from different perspectives and to look for the interrelationship of visual clues.

MATERIALS

For duplication:

- *Max's Fanciful Phrases*
- *PETS™ Small Group Checklist* for each student

- *Your Fanciful Phrases* blank cards for each student

LESSON PLAN

1. To prepare for the lesson, copy and cut out *Max's Fanciful Phrases* cards. A title card with directions is also provided. Laminate the cards for use year after year. Four blank cards are provided; make copies for students to design their own fanciful phrases.

2. Place the cards face-up in the middle of the table. Demonstrate an example with the group, but after that the students should work with little instruction. Working as a group, students should try to determine what word, phrase, or title is represented on each card. This is an active lesson with students working quickly. At the end of the activity, provide hints or suggestions for any unsolved phrases. Possible hints include the placement, directionality, or size of the letters, words, or symbols. Reading the words aloud can also be helpful.

ANSWER KEY

3. Answers are provided below. Copying the three pages of cards and writing the answers on the cards will facilitate finding the answers during the small group activity. If students are able to justify an answer that is different from the one given, that is certainly acceptable.

Max's Fanciful Phrases 1

line up backwards	jumping up and down	kiss and make up	
clean up	forget me not	Lion King	sixty minutes
pillow	blow up	ease up	Little Mermaid
to be cornered	be on time	look out	top hat

Max's Fanciful Phrases 2

right on the dot		throw in the towel
chill out	right away	Snow White
hand in hand	close call	don't mess around
left turn	merry go round	man in the moon
a moment in time	stand behind the line	Rock Around The Clock Tonight

Your Fanciful Phrases

two peas in pod	don't tease	seven seas
to be in love	three wise men	man overboard

4. Blank cards are for students to design their own fanciful phrases. Suggest that they brainstorm their fanciful phrases on blank paper first.

DIAGNOSTIC NOTES

Look for students who quickly and frequently see the phrases on the cards. Also note students who see the interrelationship between the clues, using the placement of the words. Note those students who show flexibility of perspective in order to solve a wide variety of puzzles. Look for students who are able to design clever and unusual fanciful phrases of their own.

NOTES

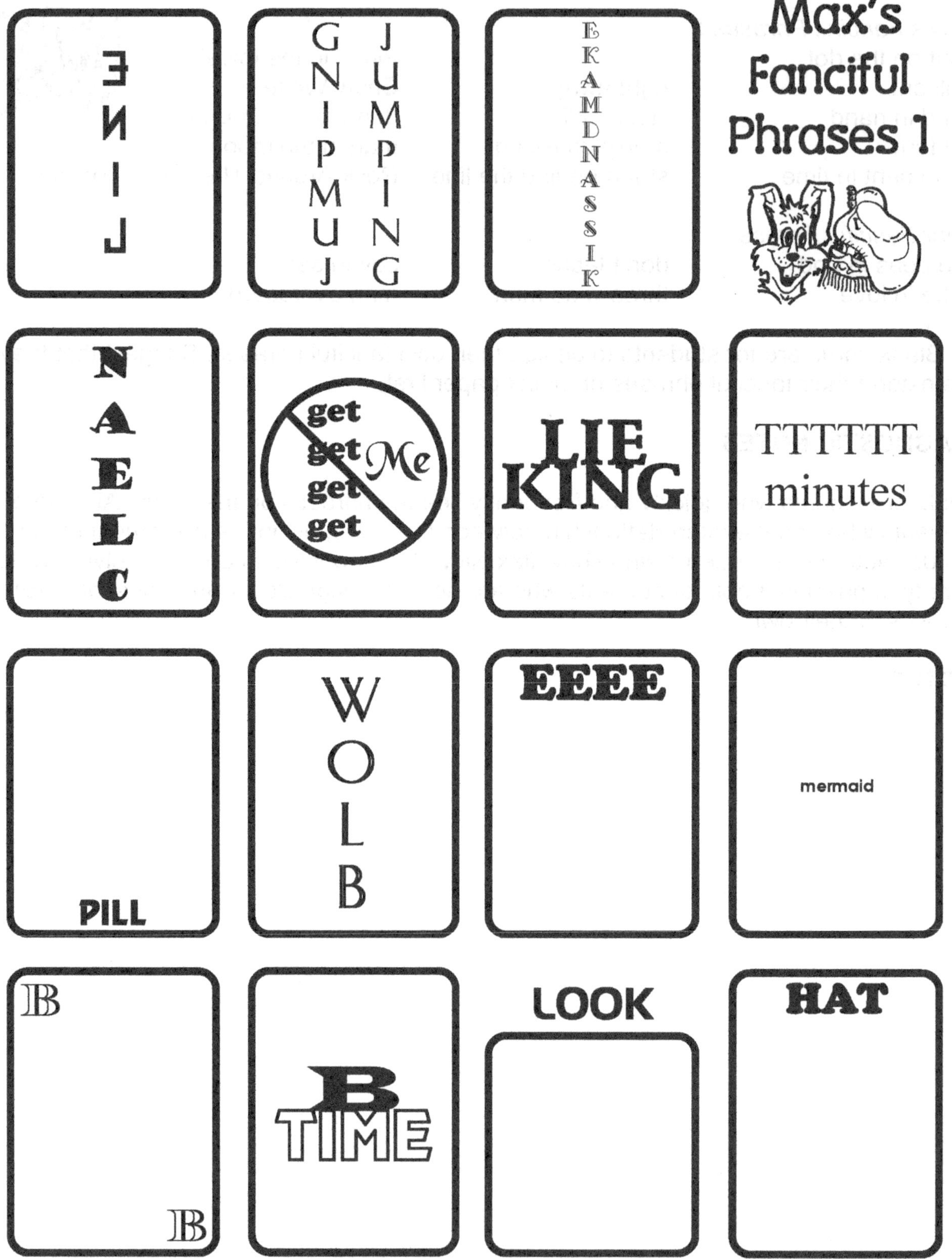
Max's Fanciful Phrases 1
JUMPING
NAELC
get
get
get
get
Me
LIE
KING
TTTTTT
minutes
PILL
W
O
L
B
EEEE
mermaid
B
B
B
TIME
LOOK
HAT

Max's Fanciful Phrases 2

RIGHT

TOTHROWWEL

CHILL

AWAY

HAHANDND

CALL

S
S DON'T M
E

TURN

MMOAONN

TIMOMENTME

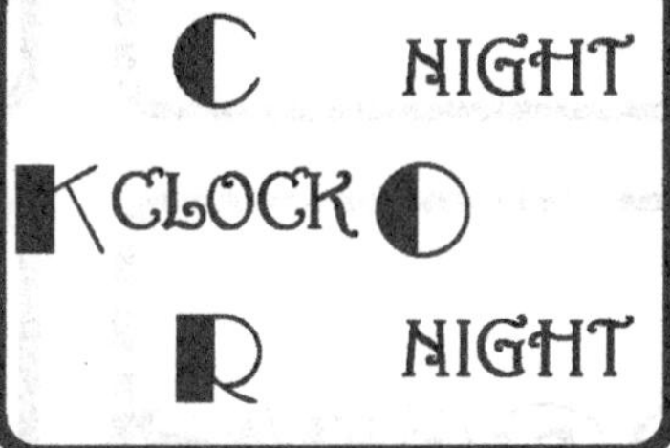

Your Fanciful Phrases

Max's Fanciful Phrases

Max has re-"written" Yolanda's favorite words & expressions.

Can you tell what they are?

PPOPD

CCCCCCC

LOBBVE

YYY
MEN

MAN
BOARD

VISUAL THINKING SMALL GROUP LESSON 3

PURPOSE

The purpose of this lesson is to give students the opportunity to use visual and convergent thinking as they develop effective strategies for the game *Numerical Quadrominoes.*

MATERIALS

For duplication:

– *Numerical Quadrominoes* for each pair or triad of students
– *Numerical Quadrominoes* game board for each group of two or three students
– *Numerical Quadrominoes Tally Sheet* for each student
– *PETS™ Small Group Checklist* for each student

LESSON PLAN

1. Prepare the sets of *Numerical Quadrominoes* and the game board ahead of time. Copy each set of quadrominoes on a different color of paper. To make the game board, copy, cut, and tape four grids together to form an 18 x 22 unit grid. Laminate the game pieces and game board for use in the future. Copy and cut out a *Numerical Quadrominoes Tally Sheet* for each student. Laminate these for re-use with dry erase markers.

2. *Numerical Quadrominoes* is a strategy game that requires students to strategically place tiles to earn points. The objective is to earn the most points. An adept player will use the shapes of the tiles to block or earn high point matches.

3. Place the 32 *Numerical Quadrominoes* tiles face down adjacent to the game board. This is the **Tile Bank**. Players should alternately select one tile from the face-down Tile Bank until each has six *Numerical Quadrominoes* tiles. Then select one final tile from the Tile Bank to be the **Start Tile** and place it in the center of the game board. *Numerical Quadrominoes* tiles have different shapes. Some are more versatile, which makes choosing tiles one of the strategies students need to discover.

4. The youngest player begins play by selecting one of his or her tiles and lining it up evenly with the same number of the Start Tile.

The player adds the numbers matched to determine the points earned and records that sum on his or her tally sheet. The tally sheet provides a column to keep a running score. Another tile is then drawn from the Tile Bank. Since earning as many points as possible is the object of the game, it is advantageous to try to match fours for a total of eight points. If a "4 match" is not possible, then matching 3's for a total of six may be the next best move. The game continues as players take turns placing tiles, counting points, and selecting new tiles from the Tile Bank. A player must attempt to play one tile during each turn, even if only 1's or 2's can be matched. If no match can be made, a player passes his or her turn in hopes that a match will be made on the next turn. A passing player does not pick up a new tile from the Tile Bank. When the Tile Bank is empty, players use their remaining tiles until no further matches an be made.

5. Players must be careful when matching two numbers that the placing of the tile does not align dissimilar numbers elsewhere in the placement.

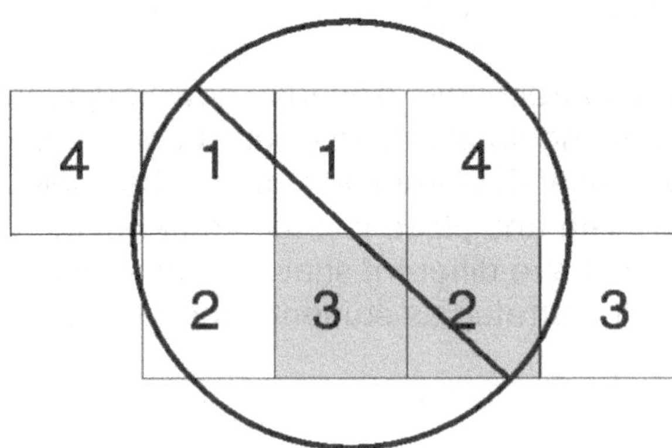

6. A player can gain a point advantage if he or she is able to place the same number with an already matched pair. For example, if two fours had already been matched and if space allows, a third 4 could be evenly aligned with one of the existing 4's on the board to score 12 points (4 + 4 + 4).

7. Occasionally a player may be able to align two numbers simultaneously on two or more tiles (a 3 evenly aligned with a 3 and at the same time a 2 evenly aligned with a 2). Then points can be taken for both matches (10).

8. The game is over when all tiles have been played or when all players must pass on subsequent turns. The player with the highest total score is the winner.

DIAGNOSTIC NOTES

Look for students who form strategies that allow them consistently to earn more than eight points during a turn. This may be achieved by adding a third number to an already matched pair or matching several numbers simultaneously or using the shape of the tile to advantage. For example, look for students who use the shape of the tile to deny their opponents access to a 4 match.

Numerical Quadrominoes

1	4		
	3	2	

3	1		
	2	4	

1	3		
	4	2	

4	1		
	2	3	

3	2		
	4	1	

1	4		
	2	3	

2	3		
	1	4	

4	1		
	3	2	

1	3	2	4

2	1	3	4

2	3	1	4

2	1	4	3

3	1	4	2

3	4	1	2

3	2	4	1

4	3	2	1

	1			2			4	
2	3	4	1	3	4	2	3	1

More Numerical Quadrominoes

	3			3			4	
1	4	2	4	2	1	2	1	3

	2			4			1	
1	4	3	1	2	3	3	2	4

	1			2			3	
3	4	2	3	1	4	4	1	2

1	4	3	1	4	2	2	3
3	2	2	4	1	3	4	1

Numerical Quadrominoes Game Board

Numerical Tally Quadrominoes Sheet			
Turn Score	Total	Turn Score	Total

Numerical Tally Quadrominoes Sheet			
Turn Score	Total	Turn Score	Total

Numerical Tally Quadrominoes Sheet			
Turn Score	Total	Turn Score	Total

Numerical Quadrominoes Tally Sheets

Numerical Tally Quadrominoes Sheet			
Turn Score	Total	Turn Score	Total

Numerical Tally Quadrominoes Sheet			
Turn Score	Total	Turn Score	Total

Numerical Tally Quadrominoes Sheet			
Turn Score	Total	Turn Score	Total

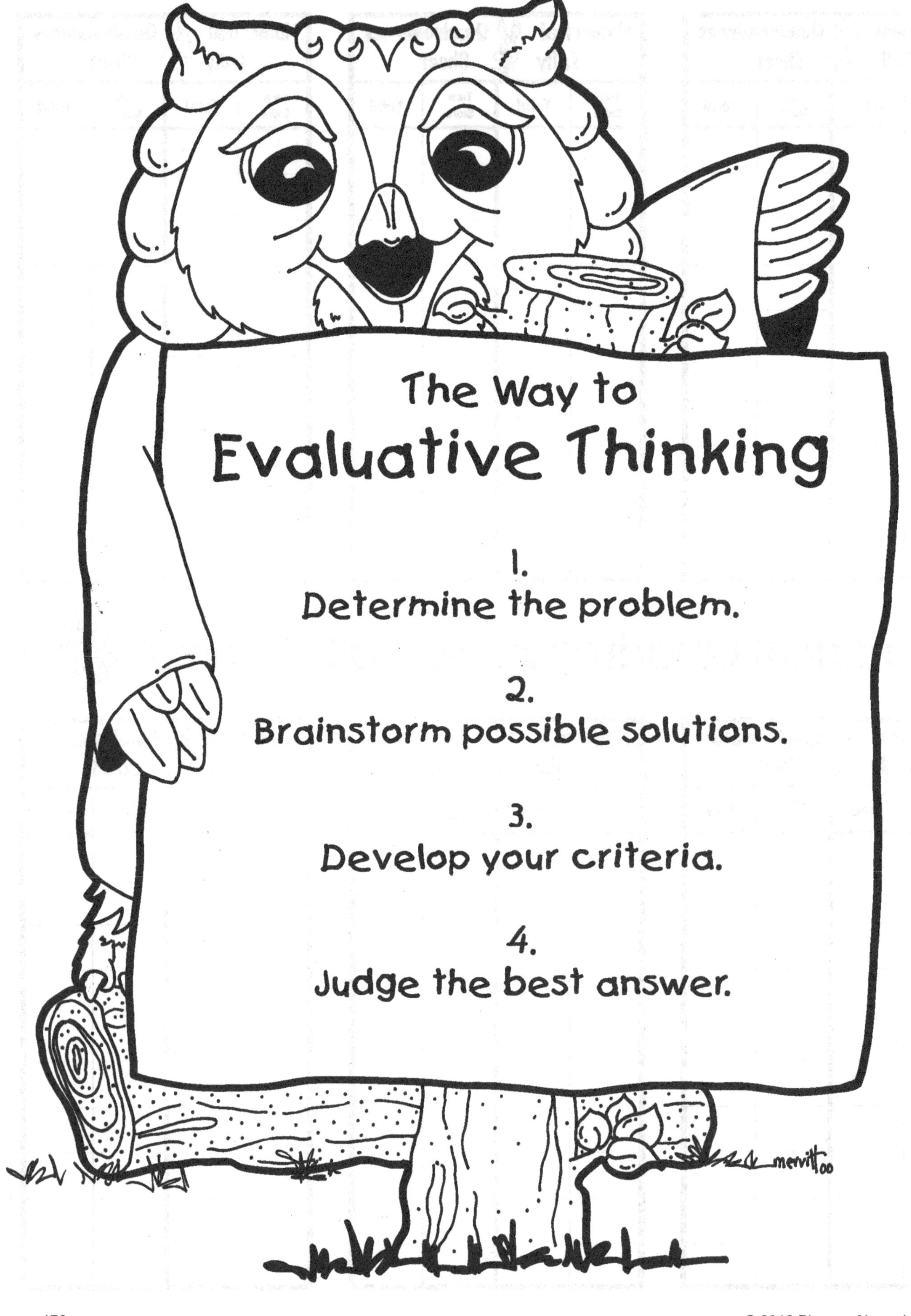
The Way to
Evaluative Thinking
1.
Determine the problem.
2.
Brainstorm possible solutions.
3.
Develop your criteria.
4.
Judge the best answer.
merritt 00

In this unit, students are introduced to the concepts of criterion-based evaluative thinking that is necessary in many daily activities and is a vital part of the problem-solving process so critical to the 21st century. In this type of thinking, students seek the best solution based on factual criteria. They determine the problem, brainstorm possible solutions, develop their own set of factual criteria, and apply those criteria to determine the best answer to the problem.

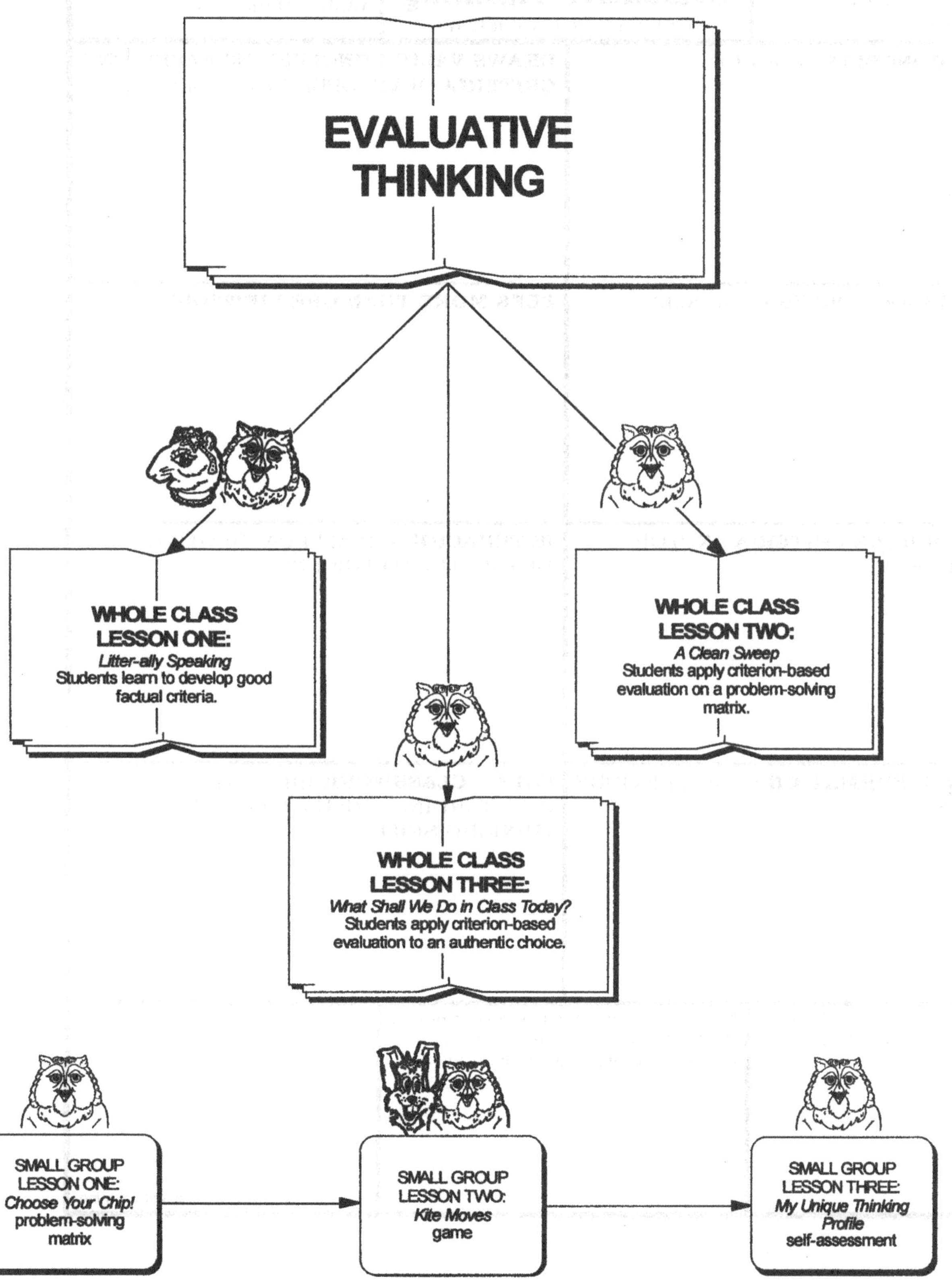

List names of students as each behavior appears. Add checkmarks after name if behavior is repeated. Use a different color of ink or pencil for each whole group lesson.	**PETS™** **Behavioral Checklist** **Evaluative Thinking** (criteria-based evaluation)	Teacher ________ Grade Dates of whole group instruction: 1. ____ 2. ____ 3. ____

GRASPS CONCEPTS QUICKLY	**DRAWS VALID CONCLUSIONS BASED ON CRITERIA** DEVELOPED IN THE LESSON
SUPPORTS RESPONSES LOGICALLY	**SEES MORE THAN ONE VIEWPOINT**
OFFERS UNIQUE CRITERIA AND/OR **SOLUTIONS**	**IS TENACIOUS** IN APPROACH; WORKS DILIGENTLY TO THE END
RETAINS INFORMATION FROM PREVIOUS LESSONS	**PETS™ CLASSWORK** INDICATES AN OUTSTANDING ABILITY TO USE THIS THINKING SKILL

I see these behaviors in these students regularly during class time as well:	These students did not stand out during the PETS™ lessons, but I see these behaviors during regular class time:	Notes:

DIAGNOSTIC NOTES • EVALUATIVE THINKING

<table>
<tr><td colspan="3">GRASPS CONCEPTS QUICKLY
♦ offers lots of ideas for factual measurable/observable criteria
♦ uses criteria to eliminate choices
♦ works the problem-solving matrix effectively</td><td colspan="2">DRAWS VALID CONCLUSIONS BASED ON CRITERIA DEVELOPED IN THE LESSON
♦ applies valid criteria to narrow the field of choices regardless of personal preferences</td></tr>
<tr><td colspan="3">SUPPORTS RESPONSES LOGICALLY
♦ states criteria used in determining solution choice
♦ supports criteria by offering ways of observing or measuring them</td><td colspan="2">SEES MORE THAN ONE VIEWPOINT
♦ sees the viewpoints of others
♦ develops criteria from other viewpoints</td></tr>
<tr><td colspan="3">OFFERS UNIQUE CRITERIA AND/OR SOLUTIONS
♦ offers valid yet creative criteria not previously stated</td><td colspan="2">IS TENACIOUS IN APPROACH; WORKS DILIGENTLY TO THE END
♦ works diligently to conclusion
♦ will NOT give up</td></tr>
<tr><td colspan="3">RETAINS INFORMATION FROM PREVIOUS LESSONS
♦ shares knowledge accurately during review
♦ applies knowledge during activities</td><td colspan="2">PETS™ CLASSWORK INDICATES AN OUTSTANDING ABILITY TO USE THIS THINKING SKILL
♦ seatwork and/or challenge papers are exceptionally well done</td></tr>
<tr><td>I see these behaviors in these students regularly during class time as well:
♦ normally great evaluative thinkers</td><td colspan="3">These students did not stand out during the PETS™ lessons, but I see these behaviors during regular class time:
♦ normally great evaluative thinkers who "hid out" during the PETS™ lesson</td><td>Notes:
♦ absentees
♦ new students</td></tr>
</table>

- *be generous — more inclusive than exclusive*
- *names can go in more than one box per answer*
- *be sure to add ✓s after names for multiple answers*
- *be sure to use different colors for each whole group lesson*

EVALUATIVE THINKING
WHOLE CLASS
LESSON 1

PURPOSE

The purpose of this lesson is to provide students with an opportunity to develop observable, measurable criteria.

MATERIALS

For projection:

- *The Way to Evaluative Thinking* signpost
- *How will we clean up Crystal Pond Woods?*
- *Our Clean-Up Criteria*

For duplication:

- the story *Litter-ally Speaking* to read aloud
- class set of *Breakfast Cereal Blues*
- class set of *Bountiful Books*
- *PETS™ Behavioral Checklist - Evaluative Thinking*

LESSON PLAN

1. Review with students the guidelines for convergent, divergent, and visual thinking. If students have completed **PRIMARY EDUCATION THINKING SKILLS 1** or **PRIMARY EDUCATION THINKING SKILLS 2**, they learned about evaluative thinking. The guidelines for evaluative thinking are listed below and are provided on *The Way to Evaluative Thinking* signpost. The term **evaluative thinking** as well as the following guidelines are presented in the story *Litter-ally Speaking*:

-Determine the problem.
-Brainstorm possible solutions.
-Develop your criteria.
-Judge the best answer.

2. Read the story *Litter-ally Speaking* aloud to students. The story instructs and models how to write measurable criteria.

CHALLENGE PAGES

Breakfast Cereal Blues
Bountiful Books

3. Distribute the challenge pages.

DIAGNOSTIC NOTES

The following is a short summary of what to look for in student behaviors and responses for Evaluative Thinking, Whole Class Lesson 1:

GRASPS CONCEPTS QUICKLY - Look for students who develop factual, observable, or measurable criteria. Note students who can demonstrate fluency in their lists of criterion ideas.

DRAWS VALID CONCLUSIONS BASED UPON CRITERIA - Watch for students who accurately apply valid criteria in order to narrow the field of many choices regardless of their own personal preferences.

SUPPORTS RESPONSES LOGICALLY - Look for students who support criteria by offering ways of observing or measuring the criteria. These students may be able to convince the teacher their rationale is sound despite initial doubts.

SEES MORE THAN ONE VIEWPOINT - Note students who see another's viewpoint. Especially notable are any students who develop their own valid, factual criteria from the other viewpoint.

OFFERS UNIQUE CRITERIA AND/OR SOLUTIONS AND/OR CRITERIA - Look for students who produce creative, yet valid, criteria. These considerations may even surprise the teacher.

IS TENACIOUS - Watch for students who want to work on evaluative-type activities. This is the most difficult thinking strategy. Note those students who stick with it and continue to think about the problem after the session. An enthusiasm towards this type of thinking often indicates an ability to use it effectively.

RETAINS INFORMATION – When reviewing ideas from earlier lessons, look for students who clearly recall the concepts and then effectively apply them to the current lesson's activities. While many children may grasp concepts "in the moment" of the instructional lesson, these students exhibit the significant ability to retain and apply new learning across time.

Litter-ally Speaking

A serious problem was developing in Crystal Pond Woods. Litter was everywhere! Isabel the Inventor's parts and pieces were stuffed in every tree hole. There was picnic trash along the paths. Max the Magician had tried to make his extra shapes disappear, but they had just scattered in the wind. And pages from *The Crystal Clarion* danced merrily across the meadow.

Jordan the Judge decided that a community meeting was needed to discuss the problem. "The woods aren't beautiful anymore," he declared to his friends. "Perhaps together we can decide how best to get rid of all this trash."

"Ideas are easy to think of," said Isabel, "but how are we going to decide which is the best idea?"

"I'll be able to help with that," promised Jordan, ruffling up his feathers and standing very tall. "I am a judge. I know how to measure the ideas so that we end up with the one best answer."

"Measure with a yardstick?" questioned Max.

"No," chuckled Jordan. "We'll measure them with words — with **criteria**."

"Words! Words! I'm the best wordsmith in the Woods!" exclaimed Yolanda the Yarnspinner.

"Yes, you are," Jordan complimented his friend, "and you'll be able to help us choose just the right words for our criteria. Criteria, you know, are the things we want to consider, or think about, when we have to make a choice between several good ideas."

Dudley observed, "I think you mean that problem solving doesn't stop with ideas. We also have to decide which idea will be the best."

"You're right, Dudley," agreed Jordan, "and our measuring sticks for our ideas will be our criteria."

"Oh!" Yolanda exclaimed. "I have just the word for what we are going to do — **evaluate**! This is **evaluative thinking**! Right, Jordan? Don't you have a list of guidelines for this kind of thinking? Where's your signpost?"

*(Project **The Way to Evaluative Thinking** signpost. Read and/or review the guidelines with students.)*

"Hey! What about the ideas? Possible solutions?" interrupted Isabel the Inventor. "We need some ideas for solving this mess first, don't we?"

Jordan agreed that this had to be the first step — brainstorming ideas to get rid of the trash and discarded treasures that were messing up their beautiful woods. The friends worked together on a list of ideas which Isabel wrote down.

*(Project **How will we clean up Crystal Pond Woods?** and go over the list with students. Students may prefer to brainstorm their own list of possible ways to clean up the woods. Record these on chart paper or add them to Isabel's list of ideas.)*

"These are wonderful ideas!" enthused Max. "Each of them is really a mini-action plan! How will we ever choose which idea or solution is the best?"

"We'll need some good criteria by which to judge them," answered Jordan. "Remember — criteria are rules or standards on which judgments can be based. In simpler terms, they are **the facts we need to consider when we make an important decision**, and they work best if they are

facts that are **observable** or **measurable** by everyone in the same way. Let's get started.

"Yolanda, we'll need you to watch how we write our criteria. Each one needs to start with **Which solution will**. We also need to be sure that each consideration is written in a desired, measurable direction. Using words like **greatest, most likely to, fewest, least likely to**, or words ending in **-est** will help us do that. Here's one to start with: **Which solution will get rid of the most trash?"**

*(Project **Our Clean-Up Criteria**, revealing only one criterion to the class at a time. The remainder of the story models the process of developing criteria needed to make a good decision. A teacher may choose to have the class brainstorm its own set of criteria and not finish reading the story.)*

"We can certainly measure amounts of trash, can't we?" queried Sybil the Scientist, joining in the discussion for the first time. "That would be both observable and measurable."

"How about time?" inquired Max. "I'm pretty busy, you know. I'd like to know **Which solution will be the quickest to accomplish?**"

"You're right on target, Max," responded Jordan, adding Max's idea to the list. "That'll be our second criterion. Anything else we need to consider?"

"Something that doesn't have to be done every day," suggested Isabel. "Write this one down, Jordan: **Which solution will keep the woods clean the longest?**"

"Good idea, Isabel!" commended Yolanda. "How about which will keep the woods the most beautiful?"

"How would we measure beauty, Yolanda? Isn't that an opinion?" asked Sybil. "Didn't Jordan say that criteria should be based on measurable or observable facts?"

"Indeed I did, Sybil, but perhaps we can rephrase Yolanda's idea so it can be measurable. What makes the woods beautiful to you, Yolanda?" Jordan questioned his friend.

"When the trees and plants are healthy and blooming, Jordan," responded Yolanda. "I think we should be looking for **a solution that will cause the least damage to our trees and plants**." Jordan added this new criterion to their list.

Max was studying the list of criteria. "Hey!" he exclaimed. "I'm beginning to see a pattern here! Look — **most** trash, quick**est**, long**est**, **least** damage! Now I get it!"

Meanwhile, Dudley was looking a bit concerned. "I know how important this clean-up is to us and to our woods," he allowed, looking around at all his friends. "We really do need to do something serious here, but I sure wish it could be fun for us to do, too."

"Then let's make that our last criterion, Dudley!" exclaimed Yolanda. **"Which solution will be the most fun for the residents of Crystal Pond Woods?** We can measure that by taking a vote!"

"Excellent work, my friends," praised Jordan. "Now we have a list of possible ideas for cleaning up our woods as well as a list of criteria to help us make the best choice. I think it's time for a break, though, so we'll take care of that at our next meeting." Rapping his gavel on the side of his tree, Jordan adjourned their first community meeting.

How will we clean up Crystal Pond Woods?

1. Recycle bins at the main entrance to the woods
2. Community litter pick-up every Saturday morning
3. Placing green garbage cans along the paths of the woods and meadow
4. Hanging signs all over the woods reminding all the residents and visitors not to litter
5. Dividing the woods and meadow into sections for each resident to keep clean
6. Paying everyone by the pound for all the trash they bring in
7. Having an Earth Day-style festival with games and refreshments that celebrates picking up litter

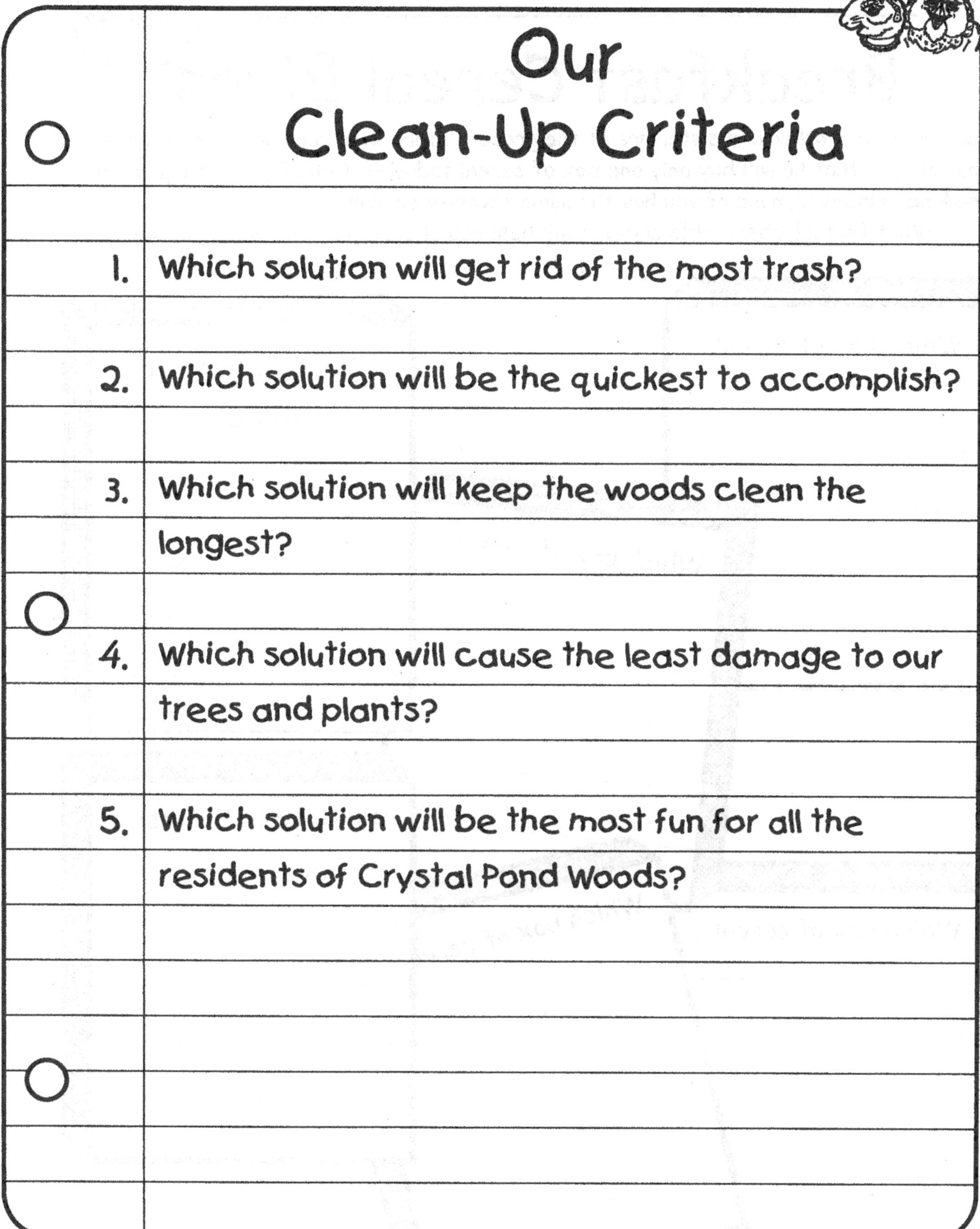

Our Clean-Up Criteria

1. Which solution will get rid of the most trash?
2. Which solution will be the quickest to accomplish?
3. Which solution will keep the woods clean the longest?
4. Which solution will cause the least damage to our trees and plants?
5. Which solution will be the most fun for all the residents of Crystal Pond Woods?

Name ______________________________________

Breakfast Cereal Blues

You and your brother and sister are at the grocery store with your parents. Your dad has told you that he will buy only one box of cereal today — if all of you can agree on one kind. However, none of you has the same favorite cereal!

What factual, observable criteria will help you choose just one box of cereal?

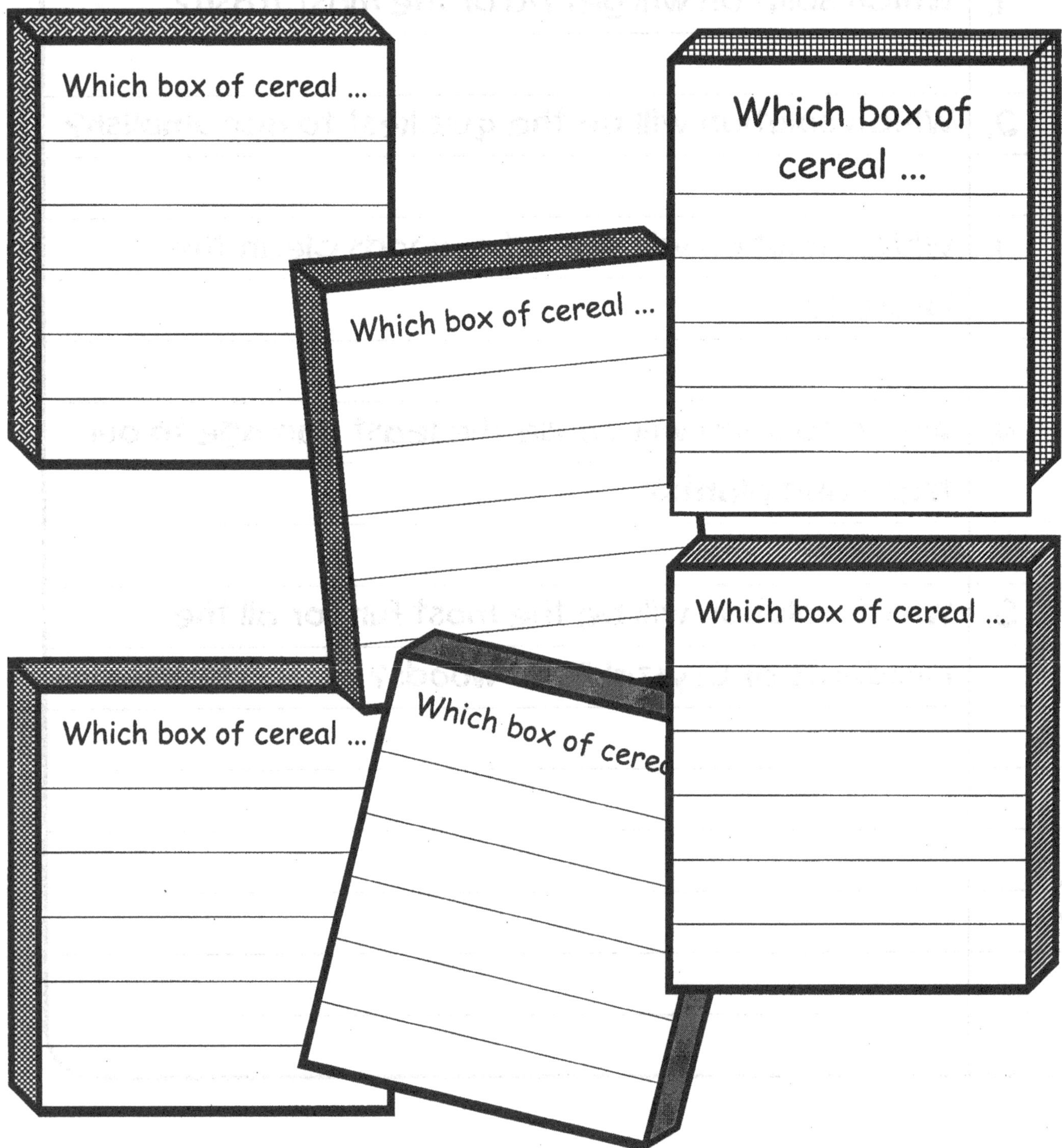

Name ________________________________

Bountiful Books

It's time to order new books for the Crystal Pond School library!
What factual, observable criteria will help the librarian order the best new books?

Which books ...

1. ______________________________
____

2. ______________________________
____

3. ______________________________
____

4. ______________________________
____

5. ______________________________
____

6. ______________________________
____

7. ______________________________
____

EVALUATIVE THINKING
WHOLE CLASS
LESSON 2

PURPOSE

The purpose of this lesson is to practice the creative problem-solving process. The emphasis is on the use of factual criteria to determine the best solution when there is a choice to be made.

MATERIALS

For projection:
- *The Way to Evaluative Thinking* signpost
- *The Problem-Solving Matrix*
- *The Best Clean-Up Plan*
- *Quiz-ical Qualms*

For duplication:
- the story *A Clean Sweep* to read aloud
- class set of *Quiz-zical Qualms*
- class set of *Where In The World...??*
- *PETS™ Behavioral Checklist - Evaluative Thinking*

LESSON PLAN

1. Review with students the guidelines for evaluative thinking using *The Way to Evaluative Thinking* signpost:

-Determine the problem.
-Brainstorm possible solutions
-Develop your criteria.
-Judge the best answer.

2. Read the story *A Clean Sweep* aloud to students. The main point of the story is that criteria make it possible to evaluate possible solutions to a problem in such a way that one best solution can be determined. Other points include:

List important known facts about a situation in the FACTS box.

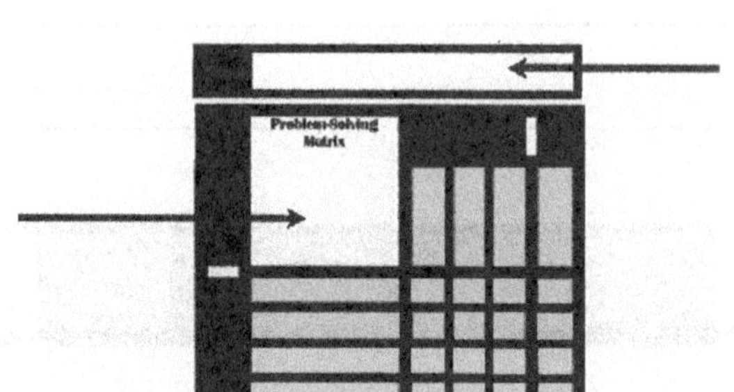

Write the established problem to be solved in the PROBLEM box.

List possible solutions in the left-hand SOLUTIONS column.

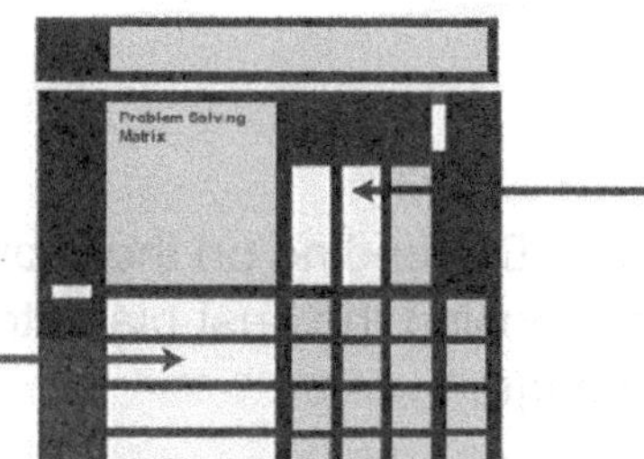

List criteria to be used in the upper CRITERIA row. Criteria must be written in a desirable direction, in measurable question form (such as **most, least, most likely to, least likely to**, or words ending in **-est**.)

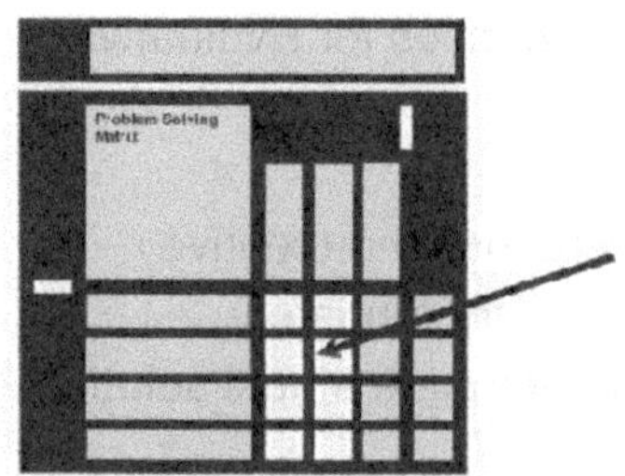

Problem-solving matrices have rows and columns that criss-cross to create cells.

Rank solutions in these cells according to each listed criterion from one (low) to the number reflecting the total possible solutions (high). For example, if there were five possible solutions, rank them from one to five.

Sometimes it may not seem possible to rate solutions differentially. Nonetheless, they must be ranked somehow - each column may only contain one of each number.

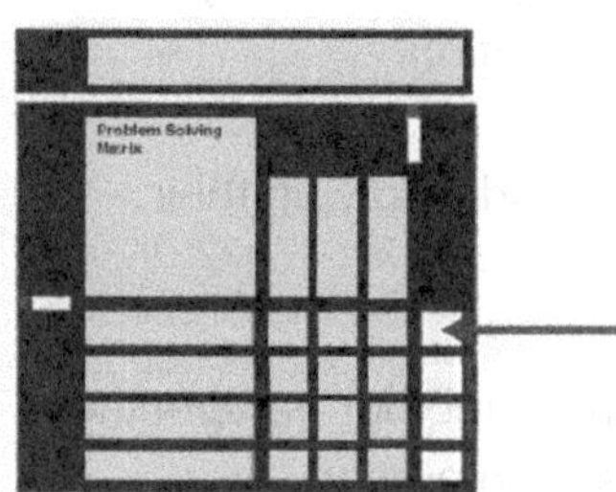

Total each row across, putting the total in the right-hand SCORING COLUMN.

The solution with the highest score is the best solution given these particular criteria.

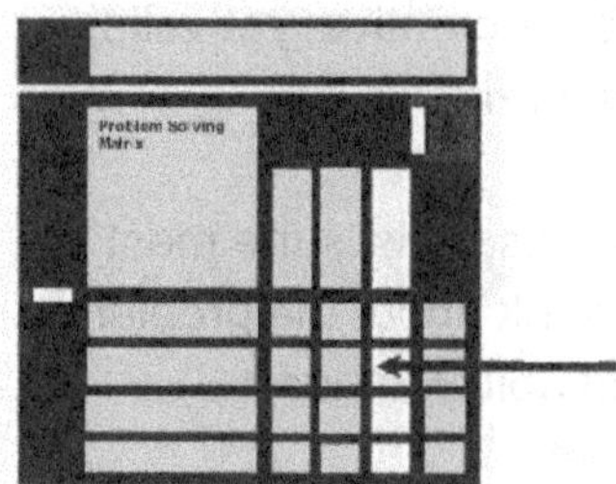

Students may justifiably disagree on how to rank solutions. When this happens, they will end up with different "best" solutions. This is fine as long as they can justify their rankings.

If two or more solutions tie with the highest score, use the shaded Tie-Breaker Column. Create another criterion, rate and rank the solutions, and re-total the rows.

3. As a group, work together on *Quiz-zical Qualms*. Have students brainstorm two or three more possible solutions (for example, **have a friend study with her, make flash cards to carry and practice with, write and memorize a poem using the new words**) and two more criteria (for example, **can be accomplished quickest, is the easiest to get organized, involves the least number of people**). Add these to the matrix. If there are five possible solutions, rank them from one to five. Students using only four solutions will rank them from one to four.

Most students will still need to follow the teacher's example, but some students will be ready to brainstorm their own solutions and criteria as well as establish their own rankings. Inform the students that either way is acceptable.

CHALLENGE PAGE

Where In The World...???

4. Distribute the challenge page to students. Depending on the group of students, brainstorming a list of possible criteria for choosing the best place to vacation might be important in preparation for this challenge page.

DIAGNOSTIC NOTES

The following is a short summary of what to look for in student behaviors and responses for Evaluative Thinking, Whole Class Lesson 2:

GRASPS CONCEPTS QUICKLY - Look for students who quickly understand and use the creative problem-solving process. Note students whose criteria are not only valid, but also appropriately directional and indicate a measure of degree. List students who are the first to determine a best solution.

DRAWS VALID CONCLUSIONS BASED UPON CRITERIA - Watch for students who effectively evaluate and rank possible solutions by applying the criteria, thereby driving a valid best solution.

SUPPORTS RESPONSES LOGICALLY - Look for students who state opinions and follow up their opinions with logical reasoning. Watch for this when solutions are being ranked.

SEES MORE THAN ONE VIEWPOINT - Note students who see the problem from another perspective. These students may also understand how the best solution may vary from person to person.

OFFERS UNIQUE CRITERIA AND/OR SOLUTIONS - Look for students who offer creative, yet valid, criteria and/or solutions that may not be directly from or related to the story or senario.

IS TENACIOUS - Watch for students who want to work on evaluative-type activities. This is the most difficult thinking strategy. Note those students who stick with it and continue to think about the problem after the session. An enthusiasm towards this type of thinking often indicates an ability to use it effectively.

RETAINS INFORMATION – When reviewing ideas from earlier lessons, look for students who clearly recall the concepts and then effectively apply them to the current lesson's activities. While many children may grasp concepts "in the moment" of the instructional lesson, these students exhibit the significant ability to retain and apply new learning across time.

Quiz-zical Qualms and ***Where In The World...??***

Note those students who use the creative problem-solving matrix correctly and complete it independently. Look for those students who not only generate unique solutions and criteria but phrase the criteria correctly as well.

A Clean Sweep

From his perch in the old oak tree, Jordan the Judge watched his Crystal Pond Woods companions gather for their second community meeting. Today they would decide what would be the best plan for ridding the woods of all the unsightly litter that had begun to clutter each nook and cranny. He swooped down to join them.

As the animals greeted one another, Max the Magician turned to Jordan, saying, "Since our last meeting, Jordan, we've used our list of criteria to shorten our list of possible solutions. We're down to five possibilities, but now we're stuck. We can't seem to agree on which of these ideas is really the best one for us to use!"

"That's right, Jordan," chimed in Sybil the Scientist. "These are all really **good** ideas. Any of them would help this situation, but how do we decide which is the **best**?"

Isabel the Inventor grinned at Jordan. "Sounds like it's again time to bring out the **creative problem-solving matrix**, don't you think?"

"Indeed I do, Isabel," replied Jordan and he drew a matrix on the ground for the committee to view.

*(Project **The Problem-Solving Matrix**.)*

"Hey, that looks a lot like my logic elimination grid!" exclaimed Dudley the Detective. "But it doesn't work the same way, does it?"

"Not at all," Jordan responded. "Let's go over the different parts of this matrix. In the FACTS box, it's important to list the actual facts that you know about your situation. The problem that you want to solve is then posed in the PROBLEM box. This column here is for a list of possible SOLUTIONS to your problem, while over here is where you would list

things you need to consider when rating your solutions. In other words, these are your CRITERIA. These other cells are where you will rate each of your solutions using each of your criteria."

"Wow," sighed Yolanda the Yarnspinner. "I think I'm lost already."

"Never fear," assured both Jordan and Isabel. "You'll easily get the hang of this. Let's consider our situation," continued Jordan. "First we need to agree on the facts and just what the problem is that we want to solve so we can write them down clearly in the matrix."

"OK," Sybil joined in. "One fact is that there's litter all over the woods and meadow!"

"And another," added Yolanda, "is this litter needs to be cleaned up."

"So let's write that information into the FACTS box like this," showed Jordan.

*(Project **The Best Clean-Up Plan**. Point out the two facts written in the FACTS box.)*

"We certainly know what our problem is," offered Max, catching on. "We need to decide what's the best plan for cleaning up all this litter that's being left in our woods, right? I'll write that in the PROBLEM box."

(Point out the problem written in the PROBLEM box.)

"That's great," encouraged Isabel. "Now let's look at our list of ideas. Max, you said we've already narrowed that list down to the five possibilities that are probably our best choices. Let's list them in the SOLUTIONS column like this."

(Point out and read the possible solutions that have been listed in the SOLUTIONS column.)

"How about our list of criteria for judging these possible solutions?" spoke up Jordan. "Let's use these four and we'll list them in the CRITERIA row like this."

(Point out and read the criteria listed in the CRITERIA column.)

"Now," announced Jordan, "we're all ready to rate our solutions using our criteria. We'll start with **Which of these five solutions will get rid of the most trash?** We're going to rate them from one to five, since there are five solutions. We will give the solution that should get rid of the least or smallest amount of our trash the **1**. We'll give the **5** to the solution that should get rid of the most trash. Max, didn't you have a meeting with a trash collector about this?"

"Yes, I did," answered Max. " I found out that according to a survey done by his company, **ecology fairs** don't result in any immediate changes. People need time to think about what they've learned. **Hanging signs** to remind people actually helps quite a bit. And while a **Saturday morning pick-up** is great on that Saturday, even better results come from a plan for **adopting sections of the forest to keep clean** since that becomes an on-going rescue mission. The idea here that is known to collect the most trash, however, is one that calls for well placed **recycle bins**."

"In that case," continued Jordan, "we'll give the **recycle bins** a **5** in the cell it shares with this criterion. *(Put a **5** in the cell that **recycle bins** shares with **will get rid of the most trash**.)* Then we'll put a **1** in this cell *(put a **1** in the cell **ecology fair** shares with **will get rid of the most trash**)*, a **4** in this cell *(put a **4** in the cell **adopting a section** shares **will get rid of the most trash**)*, a **2** in this cell *(put a **2** in the cell **hanging signs** shares with **will get rid of the most trash**)*, and a **3** in this cell *(put a **3** in the cell **Saturday morning pick-up** shares with **will get rid of***

the most trash). Now we have rated each of your solutions for this one criterion. Let's move on to the next criterion: **Which solution will cause the least damage to woods?** What did you find out about this?"

"I checked that out with our park ranger," reported Dudley. "According to him, while **ecology fairs** teach a lot, they'll also bring in a crowd of people to the Woods at one time who may *leave* more litter than they pick up! The **Saturday morning pick-up** will also bring a lot of people into the Woods at one time who may be hard to control. **Signs** may damage the trees on which they're nailed or could be discarded as litter themselves. **Recycle bins at the main entrance** will keep things *out* of the actual Woods themselves and that's good, but only as long as people take care of them. Having folks who live in the Woods like us **adopting a section to keep clean** will most likely cause the least damage to the Woods since we really know and care about our home!"

"That means that for this criterion," Sybil was busily figuring, "**adopting a section** gets the **5** and the **ecology fair** gets the **1. Recycle bins** gets the **4,** while **Saturday morning pick-up** gets the **2**, and **hanging signs** gets the **3** , right?"

*(Put a **5** in the cell **adopting a section** shares with **will cause the least damage;** a **1** in the cell **ecology fair** shares with **will cause the least damage**; a **4** in the cell **recycle bins** shares with **will cause the least damage**; a **2** in the cell **Saturday morning pick-up** shares with **will cause the least damage;** and a **3** in the cell **hanging signs** shares **will cause the least damage.)***

"Exactly," approved Jordan. "I think you're ready to continue rating these solutions according to the other two criteria on your own now."

(Have students rate the solutions using the remaining two criteria and fill in the cells accordingly.)

"We finished!" declared Yolanda finally. "What's next?"

"Now we add up each row of numbers from left to right and put the total for each row in the cell that row shares with the SCORING COLUMN on the far right," instructed Jordan.

(Add up each row of four numbers and put the total in that row's SCORING COLUMN cell.)

"Then look," continued Jordan for this was the part he liked the best, "for the solution with the highest score and circle it because, given these criteria, that, my good friends, is our best solution!"

(The story ends here unless two or more solutions tie with the highest score. In that case, continue reading.)

"But, Jordan," Yolanda sounded very concerned, "there's a tie between these solutions. Their scores are all the highest! What do we do now?"

"Ah, that's the purpose of this shaded column here," explained Jordan. "It's the Tie-Breaker Column. We'll just add another criterion there, rate the solutions again, and re-total the rows. That's guaranteed to break any ties. Try it."

(Add another criterion in the shaded Tie-Breaker Column. Rate the solutions. Re-add the rows and determine the solution with the highest score.)

The Problem-Solving Matrix

FACTS: the facts of the situation

Problem-Solving Matrix

PROBLEM: the problem that must be solved

CRITERIA: things to be considered when a choice must be made

SCORING

SOLUTIONS: the possible solutions

where solutions get rated & ranked

The Best Clean-Up Plan

FACTS

1. Litter is being left all over the woods and meadow.
2. The litter needs to be cleaned up.

PROBLEM

What's the best plan for cleaning up the litter being left in Crystal Pond Woods?

Problem-Solving Matrix — Which solution ...	Will get rid of the most trash?	Will cause the least damage to woods?	Will keep woods clean the longest?	Will be the most fun to do?		SCORING COLUMN
Recycle bins at main entrance						
Saturday morning pick-up						
Hanging signs all around						
Ecology information festival						
Each resident in the woods adopts a section to keep clean						

CRITERIA — SOLUTIONS

Name ______________________________

Quiz-zical Qualms

FACTS

Yolanda the Yarnspinner loves complex and unique words.
She tries to learn 20 new words every week.
She does NOT like to spell them incorrectly or to forget what they mean.
She is tired of taking weekly quizzes on her new words.

PROBLEM

Problem-Solving Matrix

quark quaint quibble quench quagmire quintet query

What's the best thing Yolanda can do to help her remember how to spell her new words correctly and to know what they mean?

SOLUTIONS Yolanda could:	CRITERIA Which solution ... 1. Is most likely to hold her attention?	2. Is she most likely to have time to do?	3.	4.		SCORING
1. Write the words over and over again on a piece of paper						
2. Create a fun game to help her remember						
3.						
4.						
5.						

Name ______________________________

Where In The World ... ??

FACTS

It's time for your family to go on a 2-week vacation.
Everyone in your family is going.
Since your family just won the lottery, you can go anywhere in the world!
This year, you get to choose where your family should go.

PROBLEM

Problem-Solving Matrix

Where in the world is the best place for your family to spend its 2-week vacation?

Write 3 or 4 criteria to help you pick the best place for a vacation. →

↓ List at least 4 places you would like to go below.

SOLUTIONS	CRITERIA 1.	2.	3.	4.	SCORING COLUMN
1.					
2.					
3.					
4.					
5.					
6.					

EVALUATIVE THINKING WHOLE CLASS LESSON 3

PURPOSE

The purpose of this lesson is to apply the creative problem-solving process to a real-life situation.

MATERIALS

For projection:
- *What Shall We Do In Class*

For duplication:
- class set of *A-Maze-ing Metacognition* (optional activity, pp. 117)
- *PETS™ Behavioral Checklist - Evaluative Thinking*

LESSON PLAN

1. Review with students the guidelines for evaluative thinking using *The Way to Evaluative Thinking* signpost:

-Determine the problem.
-Brainstorm possible solutions.
-Develop your criteria.
-Judge the best answer.

Then review with students the guidelines for convergent thinking, divergent thinking, and visual thinking. *A-Maze-ing Metacognition,* an optional culminating activity is on pp. 117. Announce to the class that this completes their thinking skills program and have them give themselves a round of applause.

2. Wait until someone wonders what will happen now. Point out that this is a good query as there are no definite plans for the rest of the class time. Ask if this is a problem. When someone points out that it is, remind the class that they have an effective problem-solving strategy at their fingertips and project *What Shall We Do In Class Today??*

3. Start by reading the facts in the FACTS box. Then brainstorm ten fun activities, listing them in the FACTS box. Do not worry (too much) if students list some clearly impossible activities as they are usually eliminated when students are reminded later of

the facts as they narrow down the choices to list as possible solutions in the matrix. Note students who realize on their own the limiting nature of these facts: acceptable activities must take place in the classroom (no extra outside recess) and last only as long as the class time of 30-45 minutes (no movies).

4. Brainstorm criteria by which to judge the possible solutions. **Which idea is the most popular?** is already an established criterion. Others might be: **Which idea is the easiest to organize? Which idea will get us into the least amount of trouble? Which idea fits best into the time we have? Which idea is the safest? Which idea involves the most students?** List three of the suggested criteria on the matrix.

5. Review the list of brainstormed activities. Remind students of the facts that must be considered and eliminate any that will not work within those parameters. With the first criterion in mind, **Which idea is the most popular?**, have students vote on the remaining activities. List the four top-scoring activities in the matrix as possible solutions.

6. Rank the four possible solutions from 1 to 4 for each of the four criteria. The popularity ranking has already been measured by the student vote. Tally the rankings across the rows into the SCORING COLUMN. Circle the highest score and announce to the class what they have determined is the best way for them to spend the rest of their time today given these particular criteria.

7. Spend the remainder of the class time (probably about 15 minutes) engaged in that activity. Smile and enjoy!

CHALLENGE PAGE

None

DIAGNOSTIC NOTES

The following is a short summary of what to look for in student behaviors and responses for Evaluative Thinking, Whole Class Lesson 3:

GRASPS CONCEPTS QUICKLY - Look for students who quickly understand and use the creative problem-solving process. Note students whose criteria are not only valid, but also appropriately directional and indicate a measure of degree.

DRAWS VALID CONCLUSIONS BASED UPON CRITERIA - Watch for students who effectively evaluate and rank possible solutions by applying the criteria, thereby deriving a valid best solution.

SUPPORTS RESPONSES LOGICALLY - Look for students who state opinions and follow up their opinions with logical reasoning. Watch for this when solutions are being ranked.

SEES MORE THAN ONE VIEWPOINT - Note students who see the problem from another's viewpoint. These students may also understand how the best solution may vary from person to person.

OFFERS UNIQUE CRITERIA AND/OR SOLUTIONS - Look for students who offer creative, yet valid, criteria and/or solutions that may not be directly related to the class senario.

IS TENACIOUS - Watch for students who want to work on evaluative-type activities. This is the most difficult thinking strategy. Note those students who stick with it, continue to think about the problem after the session, or even apply this approach effectively to other problems. An enthusiasm towards this type of thinking often iindicates an ability to use it.

RETAINS INFORMATION – When reviewing ideas from earlier lessons, look for students who clearly recall the concepts and then effectively apply them to the current lesson's activities. While many children may grasp concepts "in the moment" of the instructional lesson, these students exhibit the significant ability to retain and apply new learning across time.

NOTES

What Shall We Do In Class

FACTS

Today you get to choose what we'll do during classtime here in the classroom!
We have a 30-minute classtime.
You need to brainstorm a list of fun activities:

_______________ _______________
_______________ _______________
_______________ _______________
_______________ _______________
_______________ _______________

PROBLEM

Problem-Solving Matrix

What's the best thing for us to spend our time doing today?

????????

Write 3 or 4 considerations to help us determine the best activity for today's class here. →

↓ Choose 4 ideas from above and list them below.

CRITERIA

SOLUTIONS	1. Which idea is the most popular?	2.	3.	4.	SCORING COLUMN
1.					
2.					
3.					
4.					

EVALUATIVE THINKING SMALL GROUP LESSON 1

PURPOSE

The purpose of this lesson is to review and reinforce that important decisions should be based on factual criteria, not opinion, that criteria can be placed on a grid with several solutions from which to choose, and that solutions can be rank ordered to evaluate the best overall option.

MATERIALS

For duplication:

- *Choose Your Chip!* for each pair or triad of students
- *PETS™ Small Group Checklist* for each student

- five brands of potato chips, all plain flavored
- napkins or paper towels
- small container of chip dip (in case the criteria **dipping quality** is selected)

LESSON PLAN

1. Hide the potato chips and chip dip so that students are unaware of the fact that they will actually be testing the chips. This will help keep the students from getting preconceived ideas and also help keep the excitement level down.

2. Review the process of evaluative thinking presented in the previous lessons. Students will be making decisions based on factual criteria, not opinions. The criteria will be placed on a grid to provide students with an opportunity to evaluate the best overall potato chip.

3. Introduce the lesson by asking students what different brands of potato chips are available to buy in the grocery store. Discuss that there are so many brands that sometimes it is difficult to choose a particular one. Brainstorm with students the things they might consider to determine the **best** brand of potato chips to buy. Because brainstorming is nonjudgmental, list all student considerations on the board.

4. Place students into groups of two or three. Explain that they are going to evaluate potato chips to determine the best potato chip from among the brands provided. Any brainstormed considerations that allude to chips other than regularly flavored potato chips (such as BBQ or corn chips) should be removed from the list.

5. Give each pair or triad a copy of *Choose Your Chip!* Have the students select five criteria from the considerations list and place them on their grids with one criteria at the top of each column. Allow students to choose what they feel are their five best criteria. The criteria should be worded positively. For example, **"Which chip has the most salt?"** is not necessarily desirable and should probably be re-worded as **"Which chip has the best amount of salt for a pleasant flavor?"**

6. Give each group of students five paper towels or napkins and have them label these denoting the five brands of chips purchased for this activity. Then place a small pile of chips on the appropriately labeled sheets until each group of students has some of each of the five brands of chips.

7. To begin evaluation, have the students perform whatever test they devise for evaluating each chip against each criterion. Cost needs to be figured out per ounce, and may want to be determined ahead of time by the teacher. Crispness can be tested by breaking larger chips. Amount of grease can be checked by the grease spots left on each napkin at the end of the activity (this criterion needs to be saved for last). Dipping quality needs to have dip, of course, and chips are more desirable if they do not break off in the dip. Taste is always the favorite test, and there is a matter of opinion here. Try to make this as opinion-free as possible, although students most often agree on the criterion of taste.

8. As students perform their tests, they should rank each chip brand against each criterion. A **5** should be given for the best chip in each category, **1** for the least favored chip in each category. This section takes some time, since the students must debate the merits of each chip and probably have to do a lot of lip-smacking in the process!

9. When all criteria have been tested and all rankings placed in the columns, have students add their totals across each row of the grid. The **best** chip is the one with the highest overall score. Students are often surprised by their final choice because many times it is not what they claimed to be their "favorite" chip. This opens up many great discussions on the decision-making process.

DIAGNOSTIC NOTES

Look for students who see other's viewpoints and look objectively at this value-laden issue. Also look for students who support their ranking with factual information regarding the criteria. Students who name criteria pertinent to chip selection, particularly unique ones, show strong skills in evaluative thinking.

Name/s ______________________________

Choose Your Chip!

FACTS

There are many brands of potato chips.

Advertisers always want you to believe that theirs is the best brand of chips. Consumers must determine which is the best overall chip.

PROBLEM

Problem-Solving Matrix

Which of these potato chips would be the best to buy?

Write 4 criteria that will help you choose the best chip. List them in this row. →

List the different chip samples you have below. ↓

SOLUTIONS

	CRITERIA 1.	2.	3.	4.	SCORING COLUMN
1.					
2.					
3.					
4.					
5.					

EVALUATIVE THINKING
SMALL GROUP
LESSON 2

PURPOSE

The purpose of this lesson is to give students an opportunity to evaluate several different game boards of the same game to determine which game board works the best and why.

MATERIALS

For duplication:

- *Three Kite Moves* game boards for each pair of students
- *Kite Moves Tally Sheet* for each student
- *PETS™ Small Group Checklist* for each student

– a set of three game pieces for each student

LESSON PLAN

1. Review with students the characteristics of evaluative thinking. In this lesson, they will use evaluative thinking to determine which of the *Kite Moves* game boards works the best and why.

2. *Kite Moves* is a game based on tic-tac-toe: the first person to get three game pieces in a straight line (not around corners) wins. Two different sets of three colored chips are possible game pieces. The rules are as follows:

-After determining who goes first, players alternate placing their game pieces one at a time on the dots.
-After all six game pieces are placed, players take turns moving a game piece until one player gets three game pieces in a row.
-Moves may only follow a line from one dot to the next.
-A game piece cannot be placed on a dot that already has a game piece on it.
-No jumping or bumping is allowed.

3. In pairs, students should play *Kite Moves* on each game board several times. Students should keep track of their wins and losses on the *Kite Move Tally Sheet*. Remind students that the purpose of the activity is NOT to win the most games but to determine which game board works best and why.

4. Allow the last ten minutes of class for discussion. Before determining which of the *Kite Moves* game boards works best and why, ask students what were some of the criteria they used to evaluate the game boards. Possible criteria might include:

-more ways to get to the middle
-unable to get to the middle easily
-requires the most (or least) number of moves

Some of the criteria may conflict depending on student views.The most important part of the discussion revolves around the support students are able to give for the various criteria.

DIAGNOSTIC NOTES

Note students who look at the big picture by grasping the concept of the game and then studying the various boards to find the strengths and weaknesses without actually playing the game. The game-playing part of the lesson may also provide some opportunities to note visual thinking and analytical thinking. Note students who recognize the strategies involved in the placement of game pieces prior to starting the game. Although the purpose of the lesson is NOT to win the most, note those students who do win consistently. Also note students who prefer a challenging game.

NOTES

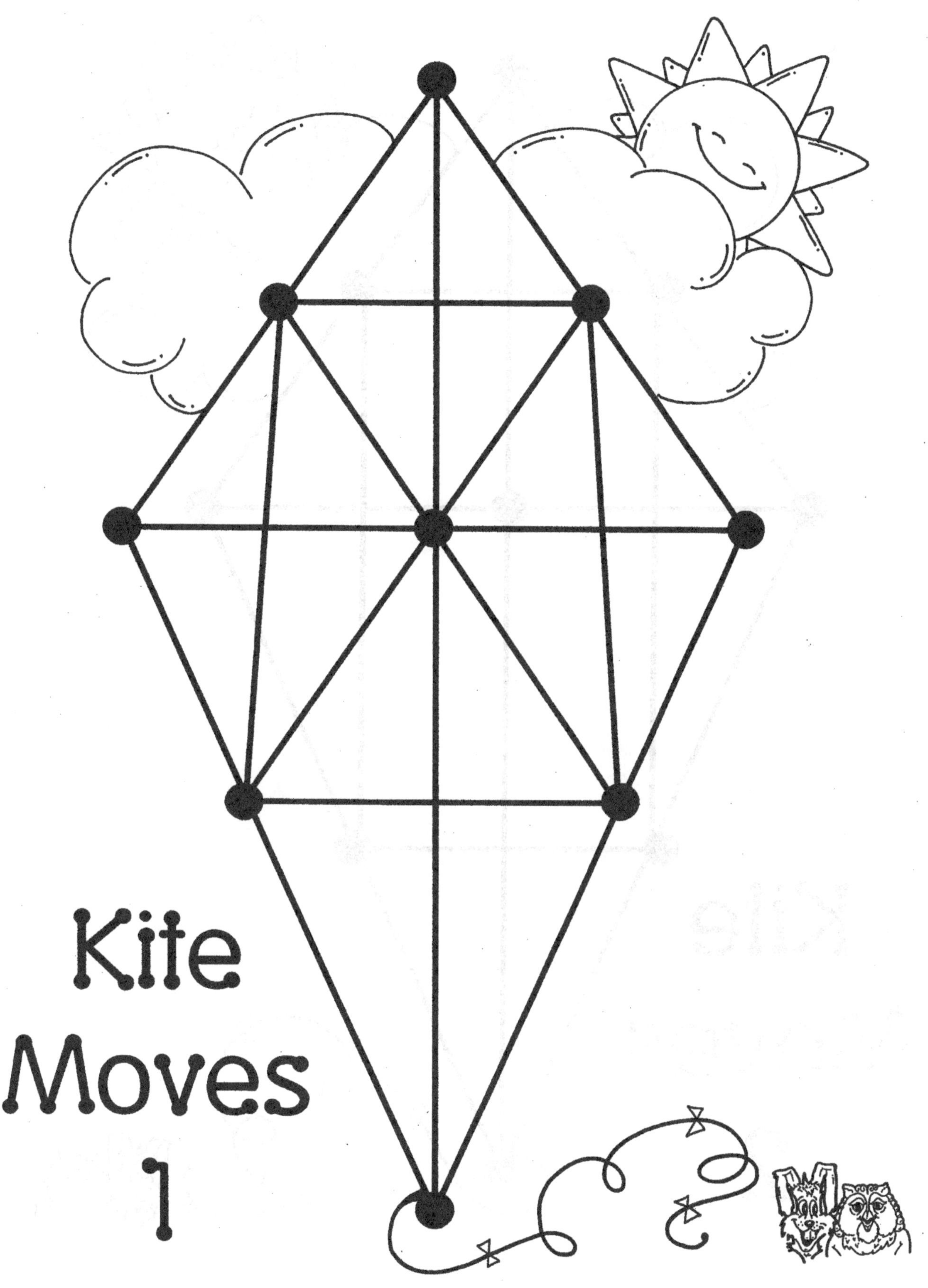
Kite
Moves
1

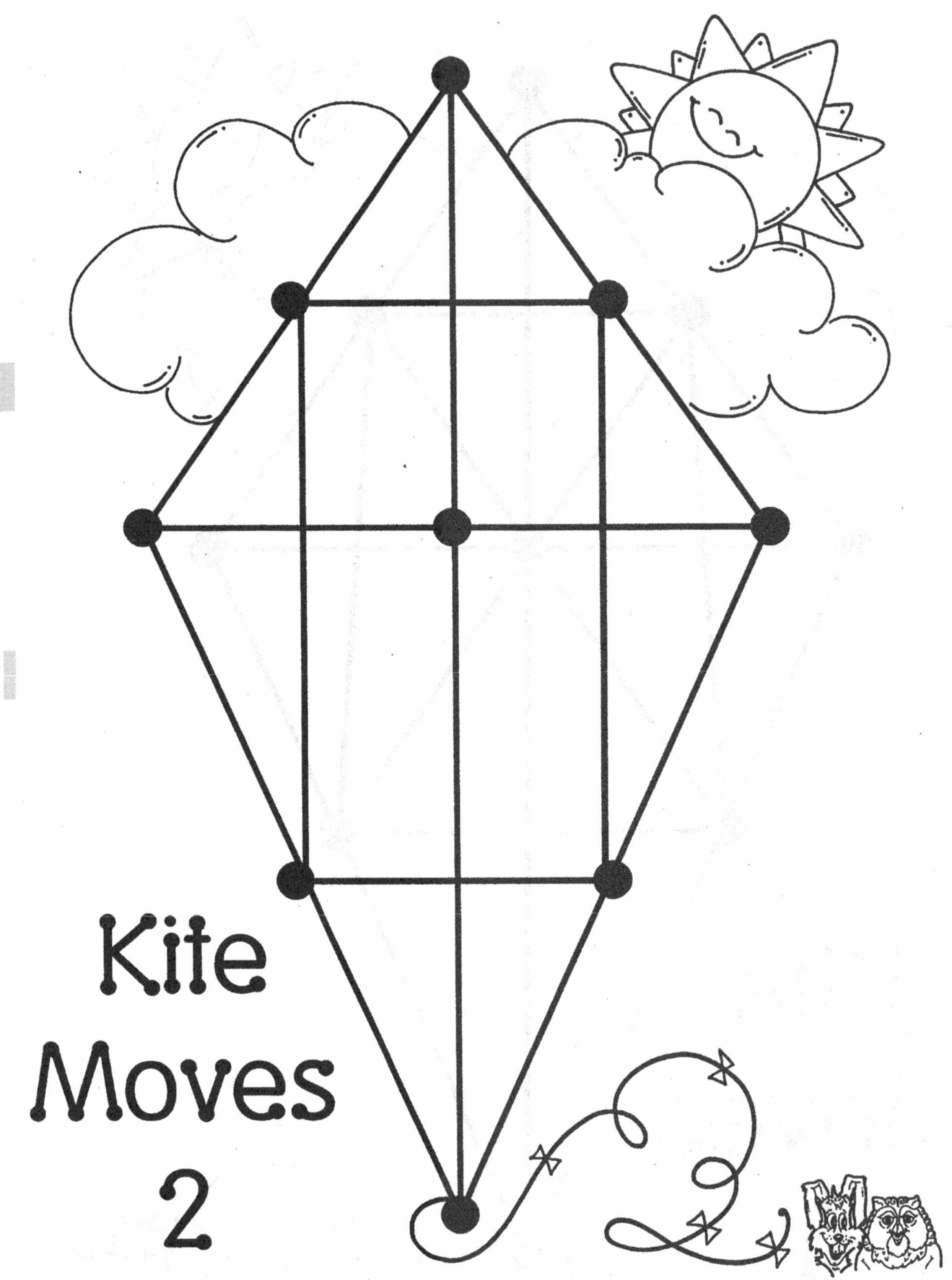

Kite Moves 2

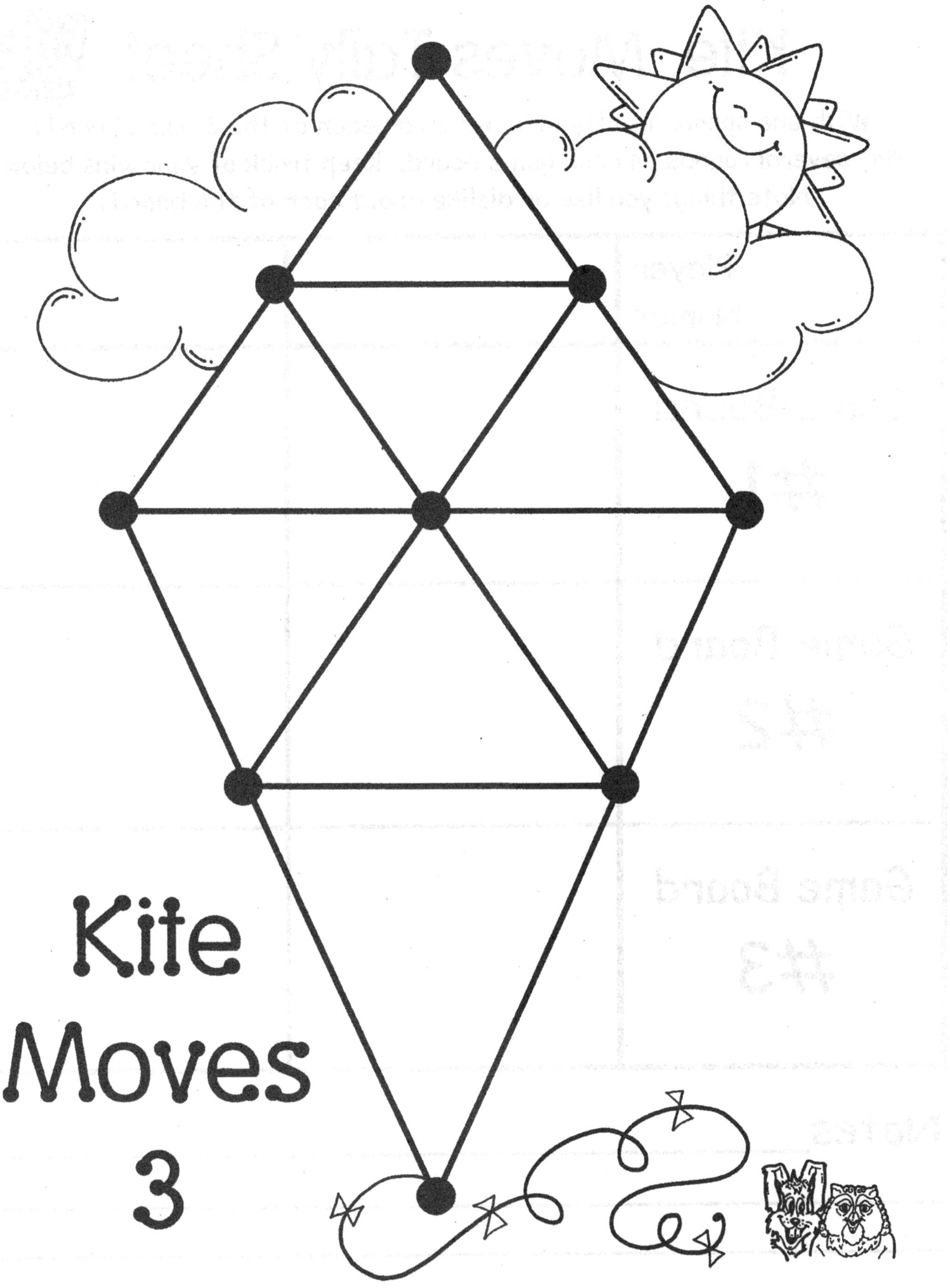
Kite
Moves
3

Kite Moves Tally Sheet

With one opponent, play *Kite Moves* on each of the 3 game boards.
Play several rounds on each game board. Keep track of your wins below.
Note things you like or dislike about each of the boards.

Player Names		
Game Board #1		
Game Board #2		
Game Board #3		

Notes____

EVALUATIVE THINKING SMALL GROUP LESSON 3

PURPOSE

The purpose of this lesson is to give students an opportunity to use evaluative thinking to assess their own strengths in convergent, divergent, visual, and evaluative thinking.

MATERIALS

For duplication:

- class set of *My Unique Thinking Profile*
- *The Way to .... Thinking* signposts
- *PETS™ Small Group Checklist* for each student

– chart paper or butcher paper

LESSON PLAN

1. This lesson is a cumulative lesson based on one to three years of participation in the **Primary Education Thinking Skills** program. Students will be brainstorming criteria which characterize the four types of thinking developed in the PETS™ program: convergent, divergent, visual, and evaluative. Based on the brainstormed lists, students will write original criteria which they will use to evaluate their individual thinking skills.

2. Write the following headings on chart or butcher paper: **convergent, divergent, visual, evaluative**. Ask students to brainstorm the characteristics of each. Record these on the chart paper. If there is a lull in the brainstorming, suggest that students refer to *The Way to ... Thinking* signposts for additional characteristics.

3. After compiling the lists, enlarge and distribute a copy of *My Unique Thinking Profile* to each student. Have students choose four characteristics which are to be the criteria for evaluating each type of thinking. The criteria should be recorded under DESCRIPTION and next to the appropriate thinking skill on *My Unique Thinking Profile*.

4. Once the criteria are written down, ask students to consider how well they fit each description. COOL, WARM, and HOT are the descriptors used on the rubric. If a student does not feel that she is very strong at a particular criterion, then COOL would best describe her for that item. Feeling that one is pretty effective at a criterion but not the best might earn a rating of WARM. HOT is reserved for those criteria at which a student excels. Students are to mark an **X** in the square to show how they assess themselves for each characteristic listed.

5. After placing the **X**'s in each row, students are to color the squares in from the first square under COOL to the square in which they marked an **X**. The final result will look like a bar graph and give a visual representation of their evaluation of their thinking abilities. At the end of the rows is a place for students to give themselves an overall rating of COOL, WARM, or HOT for each thinking skill.

6. Discuss the completed profiles with the group. Discuss individual strengths in thinking styles.Discuss ways PETS™ has helped students improve how they solve problems and areas that may still need improvement. Help students determine how they might go about strengthening their weaker areas. Discuss occupations and/or fields of study that utilize particular thinking styles. Help students realize the value of a variety of different types of thinkers in the world.

DIAGNOSTIC NOTES

Look for students who show that they understand evaluative process by writing effective criteria. Note the students who quickly disregard criteria which are nonfactual or inappropriate to a particular thinking skill. Students who logically support their responses show an understanding of the process. While the completed profiles may be used as a self-assessment tool, they should not be used as a diagnostic tool. Valuable information and insight might be provided by students but the purpose of the lesson is the process of writing criteria and using the criteria for self-evaluation.

My Unique Thinking Profile

Name:

	DESCRIPTION	COOL	WARM	HOT	
CONVERGENT THINKING					
DIVERGENT THINKING					
EVALUATIVE THINKING					
VISUAL THINKING					

PRIMARY EDUCATION THINKING SKILLS
WHOLE CLASS
CULMINATING ACTIVITY

PURPOSE

The purpose of this activity is to review some of the key characteristics of the Crystal Pond Woods thinking specialists and their problem-solving strategies after students have completed the PETS™ program.

MATERIALS

— class set of *A-MAZE-ing Metacognition*

LESSON PLAN

1. Before passing out *A-MAZE-ing Metacognition* to the students, introduce the term **metacognition.** This is what they have been doing during their thinking skill sessions — thinking about thinking!

2. After passing out *A-MAZE-ing Metacognition* to the students, explain that there are two parts for them to complete — both the fill-in-the-blank side and the maze side. Once they fill in all the blanks, those answers will lead them through Crystal Pond Woods! Some students, however, may prefer to do the maze first and then use the answers they followed to fill in the blanks. Other students may choose to use a combination of both approaches! The goal is simply to complete both sides successfully.

ANSWER KEY

1. clues
2. classify
3. find
4. reads
5. thinks
6. Brainstorming
7. considerations
8. best
9. visual
10. one
11. Yolanda
12. piggyback
13. evaluative
14. conclusions
15. divergent
16. brainfocals
17. convergent
18. Metacognition

A-MAZE-ING METACOGNITION

Name ____________________

Awesome A-MAZE-ing Metacognition!

Thinking about Thinking!

Answer these questions about the Crystal Pond Woods thinking specialists.
Then find your way through the Woods by following your answers!

1. Dudley the Detective uses ____________ to help him solve his problems.
2. Sybil the Scientist loves to study the parts of things and ____________ them.
3. The first thing Dudley does when he has a problem to solve is to ____________ some clues.
4. Secondly, Dudley ____________ all the clues.
5. Finally, Dudley ____________ about the clues in order to solve the problem.
6. ____________ lots and lots of ideas is Isabel the Inventor's favorite kind of thinking.
7. Jordan the Judge always asks, "What are the ____________?"
8. When all the possible answers are good ones, Jordan wants to figure out which one is the ____________ choice.
9. Max the Magician is a ____________ thinker who likes pictures and puzzles.
10. Dudley and Sybil want to end up with ____________, and only one, right answer.
11. ____________ the Yarnspinner loves to weave wonderful stories full of colorful words.
12. According to Isabel, it's OK to ____________ on someone else's ideas when you're brainstorming in order to come up with a bigger and better idea!
13. Jordan the Judge is an ____________ thinker.
14. A good detective never, ever, jumps to ____________ .
15. Best friends Isabel and Yolanda are ____________ thinking specialists.
16. Isabel uses her ____________ to look at things in new and different ways.
17. Best friends Dudley and Sybil are ____________ thinking specialists.
18. ____________ means thinking about thinking!

Start
classify
find
spider
sides
piles
reads
sings
knows
thinks
clues
kangaroo
help
detective
tops
brainstorming
best
see
answers
visual
coolest
considerations
evaluative
conclusions
one
piggyback
Yolanda
inventor
magician
judge
two
divergent
owl
brainfocals
scientist
friends
writer
convergent
metacognition
Finish

Convergent / Deductive Thinking

Divergent / Inventive Thinking

Convergent / Analytical Thinking

Divergent / Creative Thinking

Visual / Spatial Perception

Evaluative Thinking